The First Christians in their Social Worlds is an excellent introduction to social-scientific interpretation of the New Testament. It shows that the various New Testament documents were written for diverse Christian communities, or 'social worlds'. To understand the theology of these texts we must examine what they meant to their original readers in the first century.

Philip Esler looks at the New Testament from both a sociological and anthropological perspective. He uses the model of legitimation developed by sociologists Peter Berger and Thomas Luckmann, with its emphasis on the creation and maintenance of social worlds, and complements this with an anthropological examination of the cultural script in which the New Testament texts were written. This is in contrast to a more prevalent literary critical approach to the New Testament which focuses on the 'contemporary meaning' of the biblical texts.

The First Christians in their Social Worlds employs a wide range of biblical data and socio-political ideas to illustrate this theoretical perspective, including charismatic phenomena, the admission of the Gentiles into early Christian communities, sectarianism, millenarianism and the Apocalypse.

This fascinating study of the New Testament, examined in the context of first-century social worlds, will appeal to biblical and theology students, academics and anyone with an interest in early Christian history.

Philip Esler is Reader in the New Testament at the University of St Andrews, Scotland. He is the author of *Community and Gospel in Luke-Acts: The Social and Political Motivations of Lucan Theology*, 1987.

The First Christians in their Social Worlds

Social-scientific approaches to New Testament interpretation

Philip F. Esler

London and New York

First published 1994
by Routledge
11 New Fetter Lane, London EC4P 4EE

Simultaneously published in the USA and Canada
by Routledge Inc.
29 West 35th Street, New York, NY 10001

Typeset in 10 on 12 point Baskerville by
Computerset, Harmondsworth, Middlesex
Printed in Great Britain by Clays Ltd, St. Ives plc

British Library Cataloguing in Publication Data
A catalogue record of this book is available from the
British Library

Library of Congress Cataloging in Publication Data
Esler, Philip Francis.
   The first Christians in their social worlds : social-
scientific approaches to New Testament interpretation /
Philip F. Esler. p. cm.
   Includes bibliographical references and indices.
   1. Bible. N. T. – Social scientific criticism. 2. Sociology,
Biblical. 3. Sociology, Christians–History–Early church,
ca.
   30-600. I. Title.
   BS2545.S55E85 1994
   225.6'7–dc20 93–46433

ISBN 0-415-11121-8. – ISBN 0-415 11122-6 (pbk)

To Patricia

Contents

Preface

This book represents the revised form of eight public lectures I delivered at St Mary's College, the University of St Andrews, in the term after my arrival there, during October to December 1992. The lectures were attended by staff and students in the School of Divinity and by other members of the university and the St Andrews populace and I am grateful for the lively discussion which followed each one. Some of my revisions reflect these discussions, although for the most part I have tried not to stray too far from the form of the original.

Although originally delivered as lectures, the eight chapters published here are quite closely interconnected and pursue a common theme. I outline in Chapter 1 my fundamental approach to the interpretation of the New Testament, which is to propose (under the inspiration of the sociology of knowledge) that the various documents which comprise it exhibit a pervasive relationship between *kerygma* and context, that is, between the religious affirmations of the early Christian communities and the social realities which affected them. This perspective forms the theoretical foundation for the rest of the book, in which other social-scientific perspectives are also developed with respect to particular texts and passages. In presenting this case, I do not suggest for one moment, nor wish to be taken as suggesting, that the faith of the early church was solely the product of its social context or had no transcendental referent.

In Chapter 2 I employ the anthropology of the Mediterranean to set out the primary cultural values and institutions of the first-century Graeco-Roman East which constitute the social script, very different from that of North America or Northern Europe, in which the New Testament texts were written. Chapters 3 to 5 take up the question of sectarianism and cover, first, the mechanism which facilitated the entry of Gentiles into hitherto exclusively Jewish Christian communities (Chapter 3), secondly, the precise issue by which sectarianism manifested itself in certain Pauline communities (Chapter 4) and, thirdly, the question of introverted sectarianism at Qumran and in the Johannine community (Chapter 5). In the last three chapters I explore the theme of political oppression in two Jewish apocalyptic texts, Daniel 7 (Chapter 6) and the apocryphal work 4 Ezra (Chapter 7), and one Christian one, the Apocalypse (Chapter 8), where the question is far more complicated.

An earlier version of Chapter 3, which was delivered at the first International Conference on the Social Sciences and New Testament Interpretation held at Medina del Campo, Spain, in May 1991, has been published in *Biblical Theology Bulletin,* Volume 22 (1992), and I am grateful to that journal for consenting to its republication. Similarly, I delivered an earlier version of Chapter 7 at the British New Testament Conference in Exeter in September 1992. This has now appeared in *The Journal for the Study of the New Testament,* Volume 57 (1994) and I am grateful for its consent to the publication of the current version in this book. Unless otherwise stated, translations of biblical passages are taken from the Revised Standard Version. All quotations from 4 Ezra are reprinted by permission from *Fourth Ezra* by Michael E. Stone, copyright © 1990 Ausburg Fortress.

I am indebted to the University of St Andrews and especially to its Principal, Professor Struther Arnott, for offering me my current position and the opportunity it has provided to pursue interdisciplinary research into the New Testament. That my initiation to St Andrews was so unproblematic and congenial depended in large part upon the staff and students of the School of Divinity, especially its Chairman and fellow New Testament critic, Dr Ronald A. Piper.

Lastly, my deepest thanks are reserved for my family. It properly belongs to the genre of the preface to thank one's spouse and children for the trials endured by them during the gestation of the book. In this case, however, part of the price paid by my family, especially my wife, Patricia, was the personal upheaval of a translocation from Sydney, Australia, to St Andrews. The dedication of this book goes some little way to expressing my gratitude for her willingness to share the adventure.

Philip F. Esler
St Andrews
January 1994

Chapter 1

Social worlds, social sciences and the New Testament

SOCIETY AND GOSPEL

When Robinson Crusoe, shipwrecked on an uninhabited island off the coast of America, but having got abundant supplies ashore, sat down to consider his situation, he prepared a list of what he called his 'miseries' and 'comforts'. Three of his six miseries involved his separation from all human company and conversation. He later described his condition as follows:

> I seem'd banished from human Society . . . I was alone, circumscrib'd by the boundless Ocean, cut off from Mankind, and condemn'd to what I call'd silent Life . . . I was as one who Heaven thought not worthy to be number'd among the Living, or to appear among the rest of His Creatures . . . to have seen one of my own Species, would have seem'd to me a Raising from Death to Life, and the greatest Blessing that Heaven itself, next to the supreme Blessing of Salvation, could bestow.
>
> (Defoe 1987: 156)

His misfortune had brought home to Crusoe most acutely the need which all human beings have for the society of their fellows. He realised that to be cut off from the web of relationships, roles, institutions and values which exist among the men and women who comprise any social group is a form of death.

Why begin a work on New Testament interpretation with *Robinson Crusoe*? It is not for the reason that Defoe's classic, with its seven hundred editions since 1719, probably stands second only to the Bible in the number of times it has been reissued. Its interest for my subject hangs upon the way it presents, at least until the arrival of Friday, a mode of living a solitary existence which sharpens, by contrast, our appreciation of life in society.

For the approach to early Christianity proposed in what follows is that the New Testament documents speak to us from particular social worlds and need to be investigated using disciplines developed specifically to comprehend the social dimensions of human experience. Without this, our understanding of the texts will be unnecessarily impaired.

My position is that the New Testament writings manifest a complex interpenetration of society and Gospel, of context and *kerygma* ('the proclamation of faith'), and that we cannot hope to understand either without an appropriate methodology for dealing with the social side. The disciplines I have in mind for this task are the social sciences. Sociology is perhaps the most useful, but anthropology and social psychology also have contributions to make. I am not suggesting that these disciplines should replace the literary and historical techniques which have long been employed by New Testament critics. The social sciences are best seen as a necessary adjunct to established forms of criticism. In dealing with the past they must inevitably collaborate with history. Yet given its emphasis on the novel, the unique and the particular, history (at least to the extent it does not employ social-scientific perspectives) cannot hope to supply all the questions which must be put to the New Testament if we are to penetrate the ordinary and everyday – but nevertheless fundamentally important – interrelationships, values and symbols which characterised the early Christian communities and which are reflected in the twenty-seven canonical texts which were written for them and to them.

Accordingly, my interest, at least in this book, lies in the historical question, namely, what the texts meant for their original audience, even though the necessary research needs to be enriched with social-scientific ideas and perspectives. This is not to deny that it is also important to enquire what the texts might mean for a modern audience, or, indeed, that other techniques might be more appropriate for that enterprise. Whether this latter issue can ever be properly addressed, however, without attending to the former seems to me highly doubtful. Here I call in aid the hermeneutic path outlined by Hans-Georg Gadamer, who insists upon the necessity of understanding the horizon of the past, in our case as represented in a handful of ancient texts, in order to understand the horizon of the present. For Gadamer the continual testing of our current outlook which produces the horizon of the present depends upon an encounter with our past and its traditions. We cannot know where we are unless we appreciate where we have come from. Understanding is the 'fusion' of these two horizons, by which he means not their assimilation but their coexistence in a state of continuous interaction (Gadamer 1979: 273ff, 337ff). To understand the horizon of the past, historical analysis is indispensable.

Although social-scentific interpretation of the New Testament has been under way for nearly two decades, there are still some critics who believe that the social sciences have little, if anything, to contribute to the task of interpretation. Yet when one considers that the strictly historical methodology which they endorse is found in its essential lineaments in the writings of David Friedrich Strauss and Ferdinand Christian Baur published in the 1830s (Kümmel 1978: 120–161), this antipathy is rather puzzling. Can we really cling to a methodology in the form it took over 150 years ago, even though in the meantime we have seen the flowering of the social sciences and their robust growth and differentiation into significant new fields of research? Does the historical criticism of the New Testament documents, which were written for small first-century groups, have nothing to learn from the penetrating social analysis conducted by Alexis de Tocqueville, Emile Durkheim, Max Weber, Ernst Troeltsch, E.E. Evans-Pritchard, Mary Douglas, Clifford Geertz, Julian Pitt-Rivers and Peter Berger, to name only a few? To refuse such assistance seems to involve little more than a reflexive defence of our unfortunate and quite contingent delimitation of academic disciplines, which is itself a subject worthy of sociological investigation!

My aim in this chapter is to set out in fairly broad terms one of the ways in which the social sciences have been used in New Testament interpretation, by employing the sociology of knowledge, and to consider certain fundamental issues which arise in this enterprise. In subsequent chapters I will introduce other social-scientific perspectives which have proven helpful, especially the cultural anthropology of the Mediterranean world and the sociology of sectarianism, and focus more closely on particular New Testament topics. In the last three chapters I will take up the use of the apocalyptic genre in situations of political domination and explain how social-scientific approaches assist in the interpretation of three works, sharing certain common themes, written in such a context. This will involve a discussion in Chapters 6 and 7 of two texts from outside the New Testament, Daniel 7 and 4 Ezra, the latter being a Jewish apocalyptic work written around 100 CE (Common Era), and one New Testament text, the Apocalypse (Chapter 8), which, like 4 Ezra, reveals the reactions of a first-century religious community to Roman rule.

THE SOCIOLOGY OF KNOWLEDGE

The various New Testament critics who have engaged in social-scientific exegesis adopt, not unnaturally, a variety of starting-points and preferred theoretical positions. The area which I have found most productive of fresh questions and perspectives is the sociology of knowledge. My own introduction to the field came during my graduate studies when I began reading Peter Berger and Thomas Luckmann's *The Social Construction of Reality* (first published in 1966), subtitled *A Treatise in the Sociology of Knowledge,* at a time when I was grappling with the political material in Luke–Acts (a widely used abbreviation for Luke's Gospel and the Acts of the Apostles). It soon became apparent that the model developed by the authors in this work, concerning the manner in which a social entity is created and maintained, often in the teeth of opposition from its rivals, threw up a host of questions for which responsive data could easily be found in Luke–Acts. My discovery soon after of Bryan Wilson's sectarian typology (Wilson 1975: 9–30) and David Barrett's illuminating study of a large sample of contemporary religious movements in Africa (1968) provided a body of materials to expand the key insights of Berger and Luckmann and to generate a model covering the development of religious reform movements and sects. A little further below I shall briefly summarise this model, which I utilised in *Community and Gospel in Luke–Acts* (1987), and show how it may be used in relation to a range of New Testament documents. First, however, I should set out something of the history and nature of the sociology of knowledge and the contribution of Berger and Luckmann.

When the comparative study of religion was establishing itself as a serious enterprise in the second half of the nineteenth century, a strongly individualistic outlook was common among both British and American scholarship (Sharpe 1975: 53–71 and 97–114). Among writers such as E.B. Tylor and William James there was a pronounced tendency to regard religion as best understood from the viewpoint of the experience and psychology of individuals. In Britain a significant movement away from this emphasis came with the publication of Robertson Smith's *Lectures on the Religion of the Semites: The Fundamental Institutions* in 1889. By concentrating upon the role and importance of ritual within early society, Robertson Smith paved the way for more refined attempts to relate religion to the society in which it was located (Sharpe 1975: 80–1). Put another way, he was a pioneer in the sociology of religion. But it was in France, in the writings of Emile Durkheim, that a fully fledged theory relating religion to its social setting first appeared. His classic exposition of the social origins of religion – *The Elementary Forms of the Religious Life* (which was based on a study of the religion of Australian Aborigines) – appeared in 1912. Durkheim was influenced by Robertson Smith to an extent, but was also indebted to Numa Denis Fustel de Coulanges, whose book *La Cité ancienne* (1864) had investigated the ancient city-state in the light of its religious beliefs and traditions.

Durkheim's broad view was that a religion was entirely a product of society. For him the religious life was the concentrated expression of the collective life of a particular group. Religion was really a society's idealised image of itself. He wrote:

> Thus the collective ideal which religion expresses is far from being due to a vague innate power of the individual, but it is rather at the school of collective life that the individual has learned to idealize . . . For society has constructed this new world in constructing itself, since it is society itself which this expresses.
>
> (Durkheim 1976: 423)

Durkheim would allow of no transcendent or supernatural cause for religion; his theory was completely reductionist.

It was not till 1924 that the German philosopher Max Scheler coined the phrase 'the sociology of knowledge' ('Soziologie des Wissens') to encapsulate the insight that all knowledge has a social genesis. Durkheim, however, had been a practitioner of at least the rudiments of this variety of sociology before it had acquired a name. Yet, at the same time, the sociology of knowledge was to an extent indebted to Marx and Engels for the view, forcefully expressed in *The German Ideology*, that human consciousness is determined by social setting. The work of Peter Berger, and of

Thomas Luckmann in collaboration with him, in the area of the
sociology of knowledge owes much to these pioneers. At the same
time it belongs in the phenomenological tradition as evidenced in
the writings of Husserl, Heidegger, Sartre, Schutz and others
(Wuthnow *et al.* 1987: 8–11, 22–76). From authors such as these
Berger took his preoccupation with the role of subjective meanings in social life and with the intersubjectivity or shared
understandings on which social interaction is based (Wuthnow *et
al.* 1987: 9).

SOCIAL WORLDS AND NEW TESTAMENT
COMMUNITIES

In *The Sacred Canopy* (1969) Berger has taken the model of the
creation and maintenance of social worlds which he developed
with Luckmann in *The Social Construction of Reality* and conven-
iently applied it to the area of religion. The importance of this
model for New Testament criticism depends on the view that the
New Testament documents were, by and large, written for particular early Christian communities and that these communities
may be regarded as social worlds of the kind Berger describes.
That some parts of the New Testament – for example, several of
Paul's letters, 1 Peter and the Apocalypse – were written for
particular Christian communities (even though the word 'Christian' was not employed by their members as a term of self-
designation) is beyond doubt. My own research on Luke–Acts,
which comprises nearly one quarter of the New Testament,
suggests that its author was writing for a particular Christian
community or an ensemble of communities with pronounced
structural similarities (Esler 1987). A strong case can also be made
for many other works, including the Gospels of Matthew and
John, having had an initial audience of this kind, and this is the
view taken in what follows. Although dissenting voices are beginning to be heard on this point (Tolbert 1989; Darr 1992), some of
them at least seem to depend on views as to the original audiences
of the texts which are more problematic than the postulation of
Christian communities (see the review of Darr 1992 in Esler
1994b). Stephen Barton has recently published a helpful article
on the communal dimension of early Christianity (Barton 1992).
The notion of 'social world' has been taken up in several works by

New Testament critics (Meeks 1972 and 1983; Gager 1975; Overman 1990; Neyrey 1991).

It is desirable to offer at least a broad outline of Berger's model (Berger 1969: 3–51). He begins with the proposition that every human society is an enterprise in world-building. To explain this, one must understand society in dialectical terms: humanity produces society, yet every society continuously acts back upon its producers. Every individual biography is an episode within the history of society. What is more, it is within society, and as a result of social processes, that the individual becomes a person and attains an identity. Accounts of children raised by animals, including fictional ones such as David Malouf's visionary masterpiece *An Imaginary Life* (1980), which fuses the tradition of the wolf-boy with Ovid's exile to Tomi, reveal the vital character of social nurture for human identity. Berger isolates three moments or steps in this dialectic: externalisation, objectivation and internalisation. Externalisation is the ongoing outpouring of human being into the world, which results in all the products of our culture, material and non-material. Society is part of the non-material culture, and an essential part, since it structures our relations with our fellow men and women. Only in society can we create our world. The creation of the early Christian communities, with their distinct modes of organisation, behaviour and symbolism, provides an example of externalisation. Objectivation, secondly, refers to the phenomenon that culture comes to confront humanity as a reality outside of its human producers. Thus, the agents from the banks who come to eject Dustbowl farmers from their lands in John Steinbeck's *The Grapes of Wrath* disclaim any responsibility on their part, for the reason that it is not them nor any human beings but the banks which are responsible (Steinbeck 1975: 36–9). Here we see how an institution can acquire an objective reality seemingly beyond the control of its human creators.

Every society faces the problem of ensuring that its values, its objectivated meanings, are transmitted from one generation to the next. This transmission occurs through 'socialization', which means the ways in which each new generation is taught to live in accordance with the institutional programmes of society. From the viewpoint of the individual members of a social group, this process is 'internalization', which is the third step in Berger's scheme. Through internalization individuals identify with and are shaped by social meanings, so that these meanings become lodged within their consciousness. Thus, the institutional programmes set up by a society become objectively real as attitudes, motives and values. We are led by this aspect of the model to enquire, for example, whether the large amount of teaching contained in Matthew's Gospel (in contrast, say, with the situation in Mark) functions to preserve the author's congregation, to maintain its distinctive identity and outlook, and not just to promote ethical conduct among its members. This possibility is strengthened when the Matthean Jesus says: For I tell you, unless your righteousness (*dikaiosunē*) exceeds that of the scribes and the Pharisees, you will never enter the kingdom of heaven' (Matt. 5.20).

Here we see the notion of righteousness, which at one level encapsulates the ethical demands of this Gospel, serving a vital social function of differentiating the members of the community from its rival in the Judaism which was developing alongside it and for whose leaders *dikaiosunē* was also a key expression. The Matthean beatitudes may be subjected to the same type of analysis.

From this account of the dialectic manner in which society is established and maintained it may be said that the socially constructed world is, above all, an ordering of experience. A meaningful order, or *nomos*, is imposed upon the discrete experiences and meanings of individuals. It is for this reason that radical separation from the social world constitutes such a powerful threat to the individual, who loses not only emotionally satisfying ties to other people, but also his or her orientation in experience, sense of reality and identity. Something of this process can be seen in the experience of Robinson Crusoe. Nearer to home, for current purposes, the solemnity attached to the process of expulsion from the community which we find, for example, in Matt. 18.15–17 illustrates the enormity of such separation. The seriousness of such a step can also be seen in 1 Cor. 5.13.

Very often the socially established *nomos* merges its meanings with what are considered to be the fundamental meanings in the universe. In such a case *nomos* and cosmos appear to be coextensive. The New Testament communities which I have begun to introduce above are heading towards such an intersection. This idea can be seen with some clarity at the end of the First Gospel, when Jesus offers the fact that all power in heaven and on earth has been entrusted to him as the basis for commissioning his listeners to make disciples of all nations (Matt. 28.16–20). Success in this task would produce an *ekklēsia* on earth governed by the power of God's rule; the Kingdom of Heaven would have indeed come. For Berger, religion is the human enterprise by which a sacred cosmos is established. Influenced by Rudolf Otto, Emile Durkheim and Mircea Eliade, he describes the sacred as 'a quality of mysterious and awesome power, other than man and yet related to him, which is believed to reside in certain objects of experience' (Berger 1969: 25). The sacred cosmos is confronted as an immensely powerful reality beyond humanity itself and yet locating humanity in an ultimately meaningful order. At one level the opposite of the sacred is the profane, on another level the opposite is chaos or anomy.

Having explained the genesis of society and religion, Berger proceeds to describe how they are maintained. Here the centrally important process is 'legitimation', a word he employs to denote the socially objectivated 'knowledge' serving to explain and justify the social order. 'Legitimations are answers to any questions about the "why" of institutional arrangements' (Berger 1969: 29). Legitimation is especially important in any social order where the prevailing arrangements are under threat from dissenters from within, or through opposition from without, which may be capable of causing the members to falter in their commitment. There are many signs in the New Testament that the early Christian communities were troubled by problems whose origins were internal or external or both. In his speech to the Ephesian elders in Acts Paul predicted precisely these kinds of disturbance: 'I know that after my departure fierce wolves will come in among you, not sparing the flock; and from among your own selves will arise men speaking perverse things, to draw away the disciples after them' (Acts 20.29–30). From Paul's letter to the communities he had founded in Galatia, moreover, it is clear that the Gentile members faced pressure to be circumcised which must have been prompted, at least in part, by outsiders, most probably non-Christian Jews (Gal. 6.12–13), while internal dissensions were also unsettling the membership (Gal. 5.15, 26).

Berger and Luckmann use the phrase 'symbolic universe' to describe the integrated totality of the various bodies of meaning and symbolism used to legitimate a social world (Berger and Luckman 1984: 110–46). Where one group has recently hived off from another, for example by becoming sectarian in relation to a mother church, the need for its leadership to provide legitimation to the members, to fashion a symbolic universe within which their experience will have order and meaning, may well be acute. Berger refers to a symbolic universe in such a context as a 'sacred canopy' (Berger 1969).

Yet we must bear in mind that we are dealing with what is always a fundamentally dialectic process. Berger writes:

> Religious legitimations arise from human activity, but once crystallized into complexes of meaning that become part of a religious tradition they can attain a measure of autonomy as against this activity. Indeed, they may then *act back upon* actions in everyday life, transforming the latter, sometimes radically.
>
> (Berger 1969: 41)

A New Testament illustration of the force of these remarks presents itself if one asks of John's Gospel whether its high Christology was a direct response to the forcible expulsion of the Johannine community from the synagogue or whether that expulsion led the embittered membership to generate a high Christology as a means of symbolical compensation. The inter-relationship between the social situation of the Johannine community and the central symbolical motif in the Fourth Gospel – the descending and ascending Son of Man – is dealt with by Wayne A. Meeks in a ground-breaking article published in 1972 which employs, it would appear for the first time in New Testament criticism, Berger and Luckmann's notion of 'symbolic universe'.

One final point should be made to meet the possible criticism that this model is reductionist and allows of no other explanations for religious phenomena, in particular, those of a transcendental nature. Berger strongly disavows any such response. He writes:

> It is *not* implied that any particular religious system is nothing but the effect or 'reflection' of social processes. Rather, the point is that the same human activity that produces society also produces religion, with the relation between the two products always being a dialectical one.
>
> (Berger 1969: 47)

Elsewhere he explains that his argument proceeds strictly within the framework of sociological theory (Berger 1969: 179–85). He does not deny that the same data will respond to other modes of analysis and he carefully brackets the question of the ultimate status of religious depictions of reality.

In addition to their use by Meeks in his 1972 article on John's Gospel and in my own work on Luke–Acts (1987), these notions of legitimation and symbolic universe have recently been utilised by a number of New Testament critics. Heikki Räisäinen has found a place for them in his volume on New Testament theology (1990). Kalervo Salo, one of Räisäinen's students, has employed them in a significant redactional study of Luke's treatment of the law (1991). J.A. Overman has published a work on Matthew's community using Berger's legitimation theory (Overman 1990, reviewed in Esler 1993a). Finally, Graham Stanton has lately produced an interesting comparison of Matthew's Gospel and the Damascus Document in which he employs the technique of close comparison, assisted by conflict and legitimation theory (Stanton 1992: 85–110).

I have already begun, in the choice of some of my examples, to indicate the general applicabililty of this model to the New Testament. There are twenty-seven documents in the New Testament: four Gospels, one historical narrative (Acts), an eschatological apocalypse (Revelation) and twenty-one documents in epistolary form, some of them genuine letters and some not. At least a dozen authors are represented in the corpus. The view taken in this book, as already mentioned, is that most of these texts were written for early Christian communities which may be viewed as social worlds in terms of Berger's model. The various theologies present in them, accordingly, fall to be interpreted, in part at least, as the symbolical provinces of meaning erected by the authors of the various texts, or by the traditions before them, to legitimate the early gatherings of Christians, not yet even bearing that name. In the light of the model, New Testament theologies become sacred canopies for those fragile social worlds seeking to find a place for themselves and their faith, in the teeth of opposition from without and dissension and ennui within. Perhaps the greatest attraction of the model is that it offers us a conceptual framework for investigating the very reasons for which the New Testament texts came into existence and even the form in which they are expressed. As we shall see in Chapter 2, cultural anthropology allows us access to the social script in which all of the New Testament texts were written. It teaches us the pervasive presence and importance of the value of honour, and the very different outlooks on the family, or economics, or the use of patronage. Such a perspective is akin to knowing the rules in, say, chess or football. But knowing the rules, although essential, does not necessarily mean that one will be able to employ them creatively or to appreciate a game where they are so employed. The notions of legitimation and symbolic universe which I have just described assist one to do precisely that.

THE USE OF MODELS

A few remarks are necessary about the use of models. To some the very idea is illicit, apparently evoking the image of the arbitrary imposition of alien concepts on unsuspecting data. This objection is based on the mistaken notion that we can ever avoid employing models! Everyone uses models; for the most part, however, they remain at the level of unspoken, even unrecognised, assumptions or prejudgments which are based upon our own experience and which inevitably shape our interpretation of the texts. Sometimes an exegete's model comes to the surface. Thus, Professor Graham Stanton, in disagreeing, for good reason, with the idea of another commentator that the hostility Matthew exhibits to Jewish authorities is due to the evangelist's being a Gentile, comments: 'Ferocious conflict is often the hallmark of a close "family-like" relationship' (Stanton 1992: 138). In this case an inchoate model drawn from the area of domestic relations is enlisted to explain a feature of church–sect relations. Here at least we have an eminent Matthean scholar putting his cards on the table. We know what the model is, even if we may doubt its suitability without some specification as to what type of family he has in mind, modern European or ancient Mediterranean. Similarly, Martin Hengel has recently employed the rudiments of a sociology of sects in seeking to explain the persecution Paul conducted on the early church, but without explicating the nature or lineage of his model (Hengel 1991: 79–86).

The explicit use of models brings the interpreter's values and perspectives out into the open (Carney 1975: xiv). It also allows him or her to judge whether those values and perspectives are appropriate to the data or whether, as is often the case, they are a reflection of a late-twentieth-century worldview. At the same time the purpose of a model is essentially comparative. A model is not a set of pigeon-holes into which data is slotted. It is a heuristic tool, allowing comparisons to be made with the texts for the purpose of posing new questions to them. The texts must supply the answers, not the model. The whole exercise is designed to stimulate the sociological imagination, to free the object of our gaze from what Peter Brown has called 'the patina of the obvious' (Brown 1972: 18–20). For this reason it is inappropriate to debate whether a model is 'true' or 'false', or 'valid' or 'invalid'. What matters is whether it is useful or not, although usefulness is most unlikely without a fair degree of comparability between the model and the data under consideration.

USING A MODEL OF SECTARIANISM

The process just described can be illustrated through the application of my own model of the genesis and development of a reform movement, and its transformation into a sect, which draws upon Berger and Luckmann and the explorations into sectarianism and the formation of new religious movements conducted by Bryan Wilson and David Barrett. This particular model formed the theoretical basis of my work on Luke–Acts and a version of it was applied by Francis Watson in his book on Romans (Watson 1986: 38–40), which is notable for the fresh light it casts on a text which has been the subject of so much research. I will now summarise the model. It is very common for the members of one religious movement to become dissatisfied with it for one reason or another and to forge a distinctive outlook which responds to what is seen to be deficient in the larger institution. Often this process will begin under the leadership of a particular individual regarded as invested with special insights and powers who is able to articulate for the group the dissatisfaction felt by its members with the existing order of things and to propose an alternative path. In preindustrial societies this will often involve the reassertion of traditional values and institutions. As long as the new movement remains within the larger body it is best described as a reform movement. Over a period of time, perhaps many years, however, relations between the two may sour and pressures may build up which result in the expulsion or secession of the new group. Thereafter joint membership of both will no longer be possible. If such a split takes place in a religious context it is appropriate to call the group which has departed a 'sect'. At times the parent religion will be able to enlist the support of political authorities in suppressing the sect, since it is in the interests of both dominant church and the state to maintain the status quo.

The members of the sect, especially in the period just after the separation, will be in a difficult position. Many of them may feel residual loyalty to the church or religion they have left and they may even be under pressure from their former co-religionists to return to the fold. For these reasons it is essential that their leaders legitimate the new movement, that is to say, explain and justify it to the membership. They need to put in place a symbolic universe within which the new institutional order will have identity and meaning. In a situation where there is a great degree of animosity between the old and new groups, such legitimation may involve denunciation of the mother religion and its leadership. But the denunciation is for the benefit of the members of the new group; it is not intended to be directed at the old. The precise nature of the legitimation will often depend on the traditions which were originally shared by the two and the precise circumstances of the split.

A model like this gives us a comparative framework for probing a wide range of New Testament data. One attraction of it is that it is diachronic; it allows us to interrogate the phenomena we observe at various chronological stages of their development. If we begin with the earliest community or, rather, communities in Jerusalem for which we have evidence in Acts and in the Pauline correspondence, we will initially focus our enquiries (and here our aim is to raise questions rather than to answer them) on whether we are dealing with a reform movement within Judaism or a sect which has broken off relations with it. The former seems more appropriate, at least until the remarkable dispute between Hellenists and Hebrews in Acts 6.1 which, together with other data in Acts, indicates a fundamental rift in the early church between Aramaic-speaking and Greek-speaking followers of Jesus, and a dispute between the latter and the Jewish authorities, in spite of the recent arguments by Craig C. Hill to the contrary (Hill 1992, as reviewed in Esler 1994c).

But if the earliest Jesus movement was a reform movement of this type, what was the precise nature of the reform being advocated? What made these first-generation followers of Jesus distinctive? No doubt a belief in the resurrection of Jesus and surely at a very early stage the experience of charismatic phenomena, such as glossolalia, visions and miraculous cures, which they attributed to the presence of the Spirit among them. This experience of divine possession, which appears to have been highly unusual, if not unique, in the ancient world and played a central role in the establishment of the first Christian communities, is taken up in Chapter 3. What types of organisation did they establish? How did they legitimate them? How did theological development occur? If they continued to visit the Temple, which was itself, among other things, a mighty device for atonement – and visit it, if Acts 3.1 is to be accepted, at the very hour of the *tamid* sacrifice, which was offered to atone for the sins of Israel as a whole – how could a belief in the atoning power of Jesus' death come into existence? Did the pace of the development of distinct theologies differ between various groups in Jerusalem? Did any such differences depend upon the social or linguistic background of the members of the groups? Did some followers of Jesus manage to stay on good terms with the Jewish authorities in Jerusalem and, if so, who and why? Were the persecution and scattering of what Luke calls 'the church in Jerusalem' (Acts 8.1) something which only affected those whose 'reforms' were unacceptable to the Jewish leadership, while others were regarded as unobjectionable? If so, what was it that put one beyond the pale? Were those persecuted thought of as being within Judaism in some ways or outside it? Did the Hellenists generate an anti-Temple ideology, as suggested by Stephen's speech (cf. Acts 7.48)? If so, was this a response to hostility from Temple authorities, part of a symbolic universe created to mark the boundaries between the community and an oppressive establishment led by the high priests? Or was an anti-Temple outlook the reason why the Hellenists attracted antipathy? If so, why did they become hostile to the Temple in the first place? Did a theology of the atoning significance of the death of Jesus first develop in Jerusalem among Hellenists as part of their opposition to the Temple? If the Hebrews failed to develop an anti-Temple perspective, what led them to tread a path on this issue different from the Hellenists? These are the sort of issues thrown up by the model; more specific questions can be generated when various aspects of the model are fleshed out in greater detail.

The model suggests that at some stage breaking-point may be reached between the mother church and the new group. What form would this take in the first-century context? Most obviously, expulsion from the synagogue, a phenomenon expressly alluded to in the Fourth Gospel, where the very word *aposunagōgos* ('[expelled] from the synagogue') occurs three times (9.22, 12.42 and 16.2). But what precipitates such action? Perhaps a very high Christology might do it, given the Jewish hostility to anything which diminished the oneness of God. In social terms, however, a likely contender is the practice of table-fellowship between Jews and Gentiles in the community, the eucharistic sharing of the one loaf and the one cup, which threatened the maintenance of Jewish ethnic identity. This was probably prohibited in the first century, for reasons I will present in Chapter 4, in spite of criticism of my position on the matter by E.P. Sanders (1990), James Dunn (1990) and others. In my view, such a prohibition on table-fellowship lies at the heart of the controversy in Antioch dealt with by Paul in Galatians 2. This is the problem; circumcision and the imposition of the Law are merely what conservative Jewish Christians perceive to be its solution. The emissaries from James who persuade Peter and others to discontinue mixed table-fellowship in spite of their previous acceptance of it represent forces within early Christianity wanting to keep it within the boundaries of mainstream Judaism; in other words, to ensure that it remains a reform movement. In supporting the practice, on the other hand, Paul is propounding a course which must produce communities which are sectarian *vis-à-vis* Judaism. This is not to say, as we will observe in Chapter 4, that Paul does not have a profound theological reason for maintaining the absolute necessity of mixed table-fellowship in spite of Jewish Christian opposition to the practice.

The issue of whether a decisive break had occurred and, if so, what methods of legitimation were employed by the leadership of the Christian groups generates a significant crop of questions to put to the four Gospels. In each case there is evidence for the split. It is clearest in John, which is characterised by an intensely introversionist form of sectarianism, which I will investigate in Chapter 5. The data relevant to the matter in Luke–Acts, which I have analysed elsewhere (1987: 53–8), includes such features as the ostracism mentioned in one of the Lucan beatitudes (Luke 6.22), the intense hostility evident in the description of the Jewish attempt on Jesus' life at Nazareth (4.28–30) and the anti-Jewish passage at the end of Acts (28.25–31). The better view of the complicated Jewish–Gentile question in Matthew's Gospel is that the text, although carrying some Jewish traditions not quite consistent with its final position, both reflects a decisive split with Judaism and endorses a Gentile mission, even to the extent of advocating mixed table-fellowship. The best evidence for the former is the explicit removal of the Kingdom of God from the Jewish authorities and its delivery to 'a nation producing the fruits of it' at the end of the Parable of the Vineyard and the Talents (21.33–46, at v.43). The denunciation of the Jewish authorities in Matthew 23 is a mode of legitimation against the possibility that their influence on his audience may make their loyalties and commitment waver. The mission to the Gentiles is proclaimed at a number of points in the Gospel, most notably in the final address by Jesus (28.18–20; also cf. the use made of Isa. 42.1–4 at 12.18–21, 24.14 and 25.32). Matthew endorses Jewish–Gentile table-fellowship when dealing with the Q passage relating to the Centurion of Capernaum (8.5–13; cf. Luke 7.1–10) by adding the stray verse from Q (used elsewhere by Luke, at 13.28–9): 'I tell you, many will come from east and west and sit at table with Abraham, Isaac, and Jacob in the kingdom of heaven' (Matt. 8.11).

CONCLUSION

One occasionally hears New Testament critics who have begun to employ literary criticism in their work asserting that the texts constitute 'autonomous literary worlds', with their own rules and architecture, and should be analysed accordingly. Although this is not the occasion to explore this idea at length, it should be apparent by now how antithetical is this approach to that I have been advancing. No one should doubt that the New Testament documents manifest certain literary characteristics, especially in the area of narrative, or that the recent concentration on these features constitutes a valuable corrective to criticism which long ignored them. But purely literary works, at least as that notion was developed by the Russian formalists in the 1920s and underlies much of the talk about autonomous literary worlds, they are most certainly not. They are not literary works, disinterested by nature, and aimed at satisfying aesthetic instincts which are never easily understood but always involve the human love of imitation. Nor are they works set adrift upon the seas of Graeco-Roman literary opinion.

The New Testament texts are very interested indeed. At the theological level they are all intent on having their readers accept that Jesus of Nazareth is the Messiah. This is the case whether they say something explicitly along these lines, as John does at 20.31, or not. At the most fundamental level they reflect a religious instinct not a literary one. At the social level, they may be interpreted as the vehicles for the construction of institutional and symbolic canopies within which the communities for which they were written might find meaning in the face of a hostile world. To treat these texts as autonomous literary worlds risks betraying the experience which gave them birth.

The first generations of Christians were hauled before kings and governors, whipped in synagogues and in Roman gaols, crucified and burned as human torches. They knew persecution, shipwreck, hunger and nakedness. Their faith was at times weakened by the attractions of the world or faded from sheer ennui. Yet they also knew joy and peacefulness. They enjoyed the solidarity of the eucharist which united Jew and Gentile, slave and free, rich and poor, man and woman. The climax of the Emmaus incident, when Jesus reveals himself to his disciples in the breaking of the bread (Luke 24.30–1), is a paradigm of the intersection of the social experience and the faith of the first Christians. Most dramatically, perhaps, they knew the exaltation of possession by the Holy Spirit, and the fountain of charismatic gifts this produced. And all this they experienced within communities, where strong links were forged between social reality and theological affirmation. If we are to interpret the documents written in this situation, where society was fused with Gospel, and context with *kerygma*, the social sciences offer us resources which cannot wisely be ignored. The question is not 'Do we need the social sciences?' but rather 'How can we get along without them?'

Chapter 2

Reading the Mediterranean social script

BRIDGING A CULTURAL DIVIDE

Some time ago a friend of mine and one of his colleagues, while touring archeological sites in Turkey, were walking along a road near Ephesus. They had been looking for a particular feature without success when they came upon an old man and a young girl, presumably his granddaughter. They asked him for directions and then moved on. My friend asked his colleague if he had seen what the old man had done as they approached. He had not noticed, so my friend explained that the man had made a sign with one hand, by closing his thumb and two middle fingers while extending his outer fingers, so that his hand looked like a pair of horns, which he had pointed downwards and moved up and down. My friend's colleague did not know the significance of this even when it had been described to him.

The point of the gesture was to ward off the evil eye. This is a belief that certain persons, often characterised by crooked or cross eyes, have inherently in them a power for evil, generally associated with envy, which is likely to harm anyone but to which babies and children are especially susceptible. Strangers are thought to be a primary source of the evil eye. The old man made the gesture to protect his granddaughter against the possibility that the two strangers who approached might cast the evil eye upon her.

A belief in the evil eye is rampant in Mediterranean lands and in countries in Latin America colonised by the Spanish and Portuguese. It is today and it has been for thousands of years; it is attested in Babylonian sources, for example, dating back to the time of Hammurabi, about 1750 BCE (Before Common Era) (Murdock 1980: 58). Anyone who is aware of belief in the evil eye and the various apotropaic devices to ward it off, including signs such as the one just mentioned, amulets and certain colours (especially blue and red), will find abundant evidence of this cultural feature during a visit to any part of the Mediterranean region, from the high sierra of central Spain to the marshlands of southern Iraq. Yet to most persons of Northern European or North American descent it is largely unknown. Sometimes it is imported into other contexts by Mediterranean immigrants, but still goes largely unrecognised. In mid-1992 I saw a plastic hand swinging from the rear-vision mirror of a car parked right in the centre of the legal district in Sydney, Australia. None of the lawyers with whom I then worked knew its significance, although a Turkish friend had no such difficulty, since the so-called hand of Fatimah is one of the most common of all evil eye amulets.

Thus, although the evil eye is one of the most prevalent beliefs in the Mediterranean region, people with a Northern European background usually have no knowledge of it or its significance. Such ignorance could cause us some difficulties during a visit to the Middle East or rural parts of Greece or Spain. So seriously is belief in the evil eye and its potentially disastrous effects on children taken, that the local inhabitants are likely to be quite hostile to strangers paying any attention or, worse still, any compliments to their children. They are likely to intepret such interest as motivated by envy and as designed to cast the evil eye on the child concerned. Foreign visitors who imagine that Arab women, at least where there has been little Western influence, might share the enthusiasm of Northern European or US mothers for proudly showing off their babies would be making a fundamental cultural blunder. They would be guilty of unfortunate ethnocentrism.

The evil eye occurs in the New Testament, although it is rarely understood and often mistranslated. When Paul asks 'O foolish Galatians, *tis humas ebaskanen?*' in Galatians 3.1, the correct translation is 'who cast the evil eye upon you?' *Baskainein* is a technical word for affecting someone with the evil eye. An amulet against the evil eye is called a *baskanion* (Julius Pollux, *Onomastikon* 7.108). When Paul goes on in this verse to add '[you] before whose eyes Jesus Christ was openly displayed crucified on a cross' he is making a play on 'eyes' which is often unnoticed. There are also specific references to the evil eye (*ophthalmos ponēros*) at Matt. 6.23 and 20.15 (where the idea of envy is unmistakable) and Mark

7.22. The importance of evil eye beliefs in Mediterranean culture and their significance in various biblical texts have been the subject of recent research by John H. Elliott (1988 and 1990) and Jerome H. Neyrey (1988). Elliott has even made an interesting case for the proposal that certain material in Galatians, including 3.1 and 4.12–20, suggests that Paul, by impliedly accusing the trouble-makers in Galatia of putting the evil eye on the Galatians in 3.1, was actually countering an accusation that he himself was an evil eye possessor (Elliott 1990). Accordingly, this is an area of Mediterranean anthropology with which we need some familiarity if we are to make sense of certain aspects of the New Testament.

But the issue goes far beyond this. The fact that evil eye beliefs cause Mediterranean parents to have an attitude to their children quite different from ours raises the distinct possibility that we might find cultural differences of similar significance in other areas of human and social behaviour once we begin to look. We are all aware that when we travel abroad we often encounter profound cultural variations from our own experience. The English, proverbially, suffer culture shock the moment they step ashore at Calais. Unless our interest is a very superficial one, we seek to come to terms with these variations so as to understand more deeply the culture of the country we are visiting. Ideally, this will involve acquiring a competence in the local language. A good paradigm for this whole process is the achievement of the nineteeenth-century explorer and adventurer, Sir Richard Burton, who immersed himself so deeply in Arab culture and language that he was able to enter the most holy shrines of Islam undetected, when the punishment for such an act was death. His account of his journey, first published in 1855, still provides useful information on the Arab world prior to the onset of modernisation (Burton 1964). An awareness of the intimate connection between culture and language, however, is not just the experience of the observant traveller, since the extent to which language itself is a social product has been one of the chief preoccupations of linguistics in the twentieth century. It has become increasingly clear that to penetrate a local culture we need to learn not only the language but also the social values which it embodies and in which it is written. In other words, we need to learn its social script.

Notions such as these throw down an unequivocal challenge to New Testament criticism. The twenty-seven New Testament texts are themselves the products of a culture or cultures very different from our own. They are written in a social script which reflects their cultural contexts and which is, inevitably, quite different from ours. If we make no allowance for these divergences we risk the twin perils of ethnocentrism, of assuming the values of another society are the same as ours, which might involve blunders as serious as praising a baby to its Arab parent, and of anachronism, of assuming that another society remote in time from us shares our culture and perspectives. Our very familiarity with the New Testament texts can itself be a source of difficulty. How can something we know so well, someone might object, be as strange to us as you are suggesting? Perhaps there is no better reply to that than the memorable phrase of Jerome Neyrey: 'The hands may be the hands of Esau, but the voice is the voice of Jacob' (Neyrey 1991: xi). If we do not pierce the veil of familiarity in which we have wrapped the texts, if we do not recognise the cultural gap and seek to bridge it, we are like boorish and uncomprehending visitors to a foreign country who make no attempt to understand local customs and institutions.

Yet 'the past is another country' and much harder to get to than most. How can we hope to come to understand the culture of the first-century world in which the texts were written? Dennis Nineham reached the view in *The Use and Abuse of the Bible* that this was a virtually impossible task (Nineham 1978). This seems an unnecessarily gloomy assessment. In the last forty years or so a branch of anthropology has developed devoted to analysing the culture of the Mediterranean. Notable researchers in the field include Julian Pitt-Rivers (1961, 1963 and 1977), J. Peristiany (1965; Peristiany and Pitt-Rivers 1992) and J.K. Campbell (1964). Bruce Malina has published a concise synthesis of much of this research (1981). The principal result of this research has been the discovery of a number of features typifying Mediterranean culture from Spain in the west to Iraq in the east. This is not to say that there are not numerous local differences, but rather that certain cultural patterns recur across the many nationalites, languages and religious groupings of the region. To a large extent, the variations which occur are variations on a theme.

These patterns will be dealt with in more detail below, but they include the prevalence of honour as the pre-eminent social value, the competitive or 'agonistic' nature of all social relationships other than those involving kin, the extent to which identity is a matter of corporate and public assessment not an individual sense of self-worth, the nature of family life which embeds all females in dominant males and relegates them to the private, domestic sphere, while males operate in the public domain, the importance of patronage and, in the economic area, the notion of the limited good, whereby all goods, material and non-material, are thought to exist in finite quantities and to be capable of acquisition only to the detriment of another.

If one turns to the New Testament with even a passing familiarity with the findings of Mediterranean cultural anthropology, striking similarities between the modern and first-century cultural patterns are immediately apparent. Abundant data in each of the areas just mentioned can easily be found. Although there are some differences, they are entirely overshadowed by the sense that we are dealing in each case with social scripts which are closely related. The palm for first noticing and developing this perspective belongs to Bruce Malina (1981). Its implications for biblical scholarship are being continuously explored by the Context Group of scholars, which meets annually in Portland, Oregon, and which includes Malina, and Elliott and Neyrey, who have been mentioned already, and many others. The Context Group have recently published a collection of essays on Luke–Acts from the perspective of Mediterranean anthropology (Neyrey 1991, reviewed by Esler 1993b).

This is not to say that anthropologists have discovered any social laws operating in the area of Mediterranean culture which can be applied to the New Testament, for as Alasdair MacIntyre has argued, the existence of a number of sources of systematic unpredictability in human affairs means that no such laws exist (1981: 84–102). What this branch of anthropology provides are a set of models for social comparison and analysis which have a close fit to the biblical data under consideration. Once again, we must reiterate what was said in Chapter 1, namely, that they are merely heuristic tools used in what is essentially a comparative process. While they give us a fresh agenda of questions to put to the texts, it is the texts themselves which must provide the answers.

We all operate with models or scenarios, but they are normally unstated and may well be unconsciously infected by modern outlooks so that their influence on the process of interpretation leads to ethnocentric or even anachronistic readings. Nowhere is this more evident than in the predilection of European and US critics to discuss first-century texts in terms of individualism when that is a feature of modern Western culture largely absent from the period under discussion. So even if we freely concede that Mediterranean anthropology cannot hope to provide a set of models which perfectly match the New Testament social world, or entirely translate its social script, the alternative to their use – namely, the unreflective reliance on assumptions or prejudgments originating in the recent past of a Europe which has experienced the Reformation, the Enlightenment, the French Revolution, Romanticism, Marx, Freud, two world wars and nuclear weapons – has little indeed to recommend it.

It must be emphasised that one may defend the importance of anthropological research in uncovering the broad configurations of Mediterranean culture which feature in the New Testament, while at the same time acknowledging that the investigation of other aspects of the first-century Graeco-Roman and Jewish context also illuminates the biblical texts. Abraham Malherbe, for example, has for many years meticulously explored Hellenistic philosophy, especially in its popular manifestations, and has demonstrated its significance for New Testament interpretation, notably of the Pauline letters (Malherbe 1986 and 1987). Many of his former students are carrying on this line of research (so, for example, Squires 1993). Similarly, the recent upsurge in the study of ancient rhetoric, largely initiated by Hans Dieter Betz (1975 and 1979) and George Kennedy (1984), has been extremely useful in exposing hitherto unappreciated patterns of argument and persuasion in various New Testament texts. Nevertheless, the aspects of Mediterranean culture which anthropologists have investigated and which do surface in these documents represent that part of the context into which the populations of the time were socialised as babies and children, before ever they acquired, to the extent they did, a knowledge of popular philosophy or rhetoric. There is, accordingly, something to be said for giving this part of the context priority, since it is implicated in the primary level of socialisation of the authors of our texts and their readers. In fact, it may be necessary to understand this aspect of context fully to comprehend its other dimensions. Thus, an important aspect of rhetoric, its division of epideictic oratory into speeches constituting praise or blame, is actually based on a more fundamental cultural reality, namely, the status of honour and shame as the central antithesis in the values of Mediterranean society. To this subject we now turn.

HONOUR AND SHAME

Honour is the pivotal social value in Mediterranean society (Pitt-Rivers 1965; Malina 1981: 25–50). Honour means the perception someone has of his or her own worth and an appreciation of how he or she is rated by a relevant social group. It is a claim to worth and a social acknowledgement of worth. Like all goods in Mediterranean society it is thought to exist in limited amounts. It is either ascribed, that is obtained passively, simply by being who one is (typically, a member of a noble family) or by being granted by someone in a powerful and honourable position, or acquired, that is gained actively, through various forms of social interaction.

The Jewish interest in descent from Abraham was essentially a claim to the ascribed honour that came from having so illustrious a person as one's ancestor. This view emerges when John the Baptist quotes the boast of the Pharisees and the Sadducees: 'We have Abraham for our father' (Matt. 3.9; Luke 3.8). In the Bible, genealogies function to trace one's honour lines. Matthew is determined in his genealogy of Jesus to link him to both Abraham and David (1.1–17). He goes far beyond the honour attaching to Jesus by virtue of this descent, however, by establishing the credentials of Jesus as son of God in the infancy narrative (1.18–2.23), even though the title itself is not used in this section of the First Gospel.

Too little attention has been paid in discussions of New Testament Christology to the question of how Jesus' honour is promoted by the various ways in which he is described. Ascribed honour of the first type is present in those parts of the New Testament which speak of the preexistence of Jesus, especially as divine son or divine Wisdom, or at least go close to speaking of him in these terms, for example, in 1 Cor. 1.24, Col. 1.15–17, Heb. 1.1–4 and John 1.1–18. In the Hebrews passage just cited the author presents Jesus as the one in whom God's Wisdom, Word and Son are definitively expressed (Lindars 1991: 33).

The best examples of ascribed honour in the second sense, where it is granted to someone, may be found in the descriptions

of the exaltation of Jesus by the Father as a result of his death and
resurrection. This grant of honour is very significant when one
recollects that crucifixion was the most dishonourable of all
deaths; indeed it may be described in the parlance of contemporary sociology as a status degradation ritual (Malina and Neyrey
1991: 107). For the first Christians a great paradox of their faith
was that Jesus could have undergone so shameful a death and yet
have achieved thereby undying glory, that is, honour. Both these
elements are brought together in Philippians: 'he humbled himself and became obedient, unto death, even death on a cross!
Therefore God has highly exalted him and bestowed on him the
name which is above every name' (Phil. 2.8–9). They also occur
together of Jesus in Heb. 12.2: 'who, for the joy that was set before
him endured the cross, despising the shame, and is seated at the
right hand of the throne of God'. Sometimes the honour of Jesus
is described in terms in which the distinction between the two
types is somewhat blurred. Thus it is not always clear whether the
pervasive references to Jesus as divine son reflect his ascribed
status as a preexistent being or are based on a gift by the Father
consequent upon his passion and exaltation. There is, however,
no doubt of the honour which he acquires as divine son, especially
to the extent that such honour makes him superior to others, for
example, the angels and Moses in Hebrews 1–3.

An important aspect of ascribed honour is that the family of
the person so honoured share in his or her honour. This is an
aspect of the strongly corporate nature of Mediterranean society
(Malina 1981: 51–70). A good example occurs in the description
of the elevation of Eliakim as comptroller of the royal household
during the reign of Hezekiah in Isa. 22.20–24: 'He will be a seat of
honour for his father's family . . . On him will hang the whole
glory of the family, even to the meanest members – all the
paltriest of vessels, whether bowl or pot' (v.24; *The Revised English
Bible [REB]*). Such a perspective means that the early Christian
communities would have regarded themselves as sharing in the
glory ascribed to Jesus by God as a result of his passion and
resurrection. The crucial Pauline notion of participation in
Christ, even to the extent of dying and rising with him (cf. Rom
6.3–4), carries this flavour. The author of Hebrews, moreover,
actually exhorts the followers of Jesus to share his shame so that
they might also enjoy his glory: 'Therefore let us go forth to him
outside the camp, and bear the abuse he endured. For here we

have no lasting city, but we seek the city which is to come' (Heb. 12.13–4).

Acquired honour is the socially recognised claim to worth which a person earns by excelling over others in various forms of social interaction. In Mediterranean society a line is drawn between those who are one's kin, or fictive kin (for example, the members of the early Christian communities or those in a patron–client relationship), and those who are not. Between kin and fictive kin exist trust, confidence and unselfish assistance. The frequent appearance in the New Testament of the notion that the followers of Jesus are brothers and sisters with the one Father is a way of appropriating to the life of the communities the most powerful corporate symbol in this culture – the family. To those who are not kin, however, a very different attitude prevails, not merely with relationships being governed by self-interest but with the objective of obtaining honour by vanquishing or even deceiving non-kin in any possible situation. It is possible that the apparently strange behaviour of Jesus in John 7.1–10, where he tells his brothers that he is not going up to Jerusalem and then goes up secretly, reflects this outlook. He appears to be treating them as one would be entitled to treat non-kin in this culture for the reason that by not believing in him (7.5) they have forfeited the claims of kinship.

Virtually any form of social intercourse – gift-giving, dinner invitations, discussions in public places, buying and selling, arranging marriages and any form of agreements on matters of common interest – opens up to the participants an opportunity to enhance one's honour at the expense of someone else. The degree to which competitiveness characterises this culture has led anthropologists to refer to it as 'agonistic' (Peristiany 1965: 14). Again, this is a feature of Mediterranean society as alien to most Northern Europeans as the evil eye and yet it is a cultural feature of fundamental importance. The New Testament is full of examples, most obviously the controversies in which Jesus engages with various Jewish opponents. The fact that he wins would have been construed as enhancing his honour and, moreover, that of his followers, his fictive kin.

The process whereby honour is acquired can usually be analysed in terms of the process known as 'challenge and response', as explained by Bourdieu in his seminal essay on the phenomenon (Bourdieu 1965; also see Malina 1981: 30–9). This process occurs in four stages. First there is the challenge, which consists of a claim to enter the social space of another. The claim may be either positive, to gain a share in that space or at least a co-operative and mutually beneficial foothold, or negative, to dislodge another from his or her social space. The challenge may be issued by word or deed or both. A positive challenge will start with a word of praise, a gift or a sincere request for help, while a negative challenge will commence with an insult, a threat or a physical affront. An ambiguous challenge will leave its target in doubt as to whether an insult is intended or not: 'Demetrios tells me your daughter is a whore.' A good example appears in the question of the Johannine Jesus: 'If you continue in my word, you are truly my disciples, and you will know the truth and the truth will make you free' (John 8.31). The Jews listening to Jesus regarded this as an insult and therefore as a challenge: 'We are descendants of Abraham, and have never been in bondage to anyone. How is it that you say, "You will be made free?"' (John 8.33). The second stage is how the challenge is perceived. This is a game that only equals can play, since only an equal can challenge another in such a way that all perceive the interaction as a challenge. Assuming this is the case, the receiver must judge the challenge in terms of the harm it will cause his or her honour if it goes unanswered. The third stage is the receiver's response. There are three possibilities: first, a positive refusal to act, for example by scorn or disdain; secondly, acceptance of the challenge, coupled with a counter-challenge, either positive or negative; and, thirdly, negative refusal to act, which may imply dishonour. The public verdict is the fourth stage in the process of challenge and response. This is a social engagement fought out before an audience whose approval is sought by each of the participants. The public verdict may be either a grant of honour taken from the person who receives the challenge and awarded to the successful challenger, or a loss of honour to the challenger in favour of the recipient.

The controversy over Abraham in John 8.31–59, the opening of which was just mentioned, can be analysed in its entirety in terms of challenge and response and I will return to this passage in Chapter 5. A shorter and more straightforward example of the process may be seen in the discussion of Jesus' authority in Mark 11.27–33. The question of the high priests, scribes and elders as to the basis of his authority is a challenge to Jesus' honour, a claim to enter his social space and to dislodge him from it. Jesus perceives it as such, accepts the challenge and issues a counter-challenge: 'Was the baptism of John from God or men?' (v.30). This cleverly throws his challengers into a dilemma, as they are unable to answer the question safely. Accordingly, they answer 'We do not know', a feeble and therefore dishonourable reply. Jesus then concludes the exchange by saying he will not answer their question. A public verdict in favour of Jesus is implied in this exchange. The same is the case with the not dissimilar pericope in Mark concerning Caesar's tax (Mark 12.13–17). Luke adds to his version of this passage an explicit statement to the effect that Jesus' Jewish interlocutors failed in their attempt to catch him out in what he said 'in the presence of the people' (Luke 20.26). This addition brings out the fact that the exchange is deliberately provoked to influence public opinion against Jesus, to diminish his honour, which would be implicit in any event.

DYADIC PERSONALITY

One of the spectacles of the opening ceremony of the Olympic Games in Barcelona in 1992 was the erection of castells. These were pyramids of men and boys organised in teams wearing distinctive colours who stood on one another's shoulders until the whole edifice had reached a dizzying height. Castells are local cultural events and the teams engage in competition to see who can achieve the greatest elevation. They nicely illustrate a feature of Mediterranean social life having far wider connotations. The emphasis on honour in this culture is related to the manner in which personality is perceived. Since honour, the pivotal social good, depends upon a grant of public approval, the extent to which a person's sense of self is dependent upon the perception of others is far greater than in the case of Northern European and North American contexts. Similarly, the tendency for persons to assess themselves on the basis of intrinsic worth, whatever the world may think, is uncommon in Mediterranean culture, at least in the absence of North American or Northern European influence. Individualism as we know it is also unusual. Persons are not oriented towards themselves as individuals, but towards the groups to which they belong. Everyone finds a place in society by being embedded in one or more groups, such as the family, which is by far the most important, and in craft associations, religious cults or even military units. The castells of Barcelona are a

modern example. This type of personality is referred to as
'dyadic' (Malina 1981: 51–70).

One consequence of this perspective on personality is that
human behaviour does not tend to be explained in uniquely
personal or introspective terms. Rather, people are accounted for
on the basis of the groups to which they belong. This results in
classification by stereotypes. Jesus fell foul of these at Nazareth: 'Is
this not the carpenter, the son of Mary and brother of James and
Joses and Judas and Simon, and are not his sisters here with us?'
(Mark 6.3). Judgement according to birthplace emerges in
Nathanael's remark to him 'Can anything good come out of
Nazareth?' (John 1.46) and in the saying in Titus 1.12: 'Cretans
are always liars.' Judgement was also made on the basis of race:
'Jews have no dealings with Samaritans' (John 4.9).

Bruce Malina has suggested an interesting view of what conscience means in this context. Pointing to the etymology of both
conscientia in Latin and *suneidesis* in Greek as 'with-knowledge',
that is a knowledge with others, individualised common knowledge, he comments:

> Conscience then refers to a person's sensitive awareness to his
> public ego-image with the purpose of striving to align his own
> personal behaviour and self-assessment with that publicly per-
> ceived ego-image. A person with a conscience is a respectable,
> reputable, and honorable person.
>
> (1981: 51)

This view meshes closely with recent discussion on the nature of
Paul's conscience. Many New Testament critics have accepted the
arguments of Krister Stendahl that Paul, unlike Luther, was not
tormented by an agonised conscience and that the type of conscience which characterised the young Luther was actually a post-
biblical development, stemming in part from the style of personal
assessment carried out by Augustine in his *Confessions* (Stendahl
1963). Malina's proposal provides support for this view, by allowing us to situate Paul's conscience more firmly than hitherto
appreciated in the Mediterranean culture of his day, prior to the
development of 'the introspective conscience of the West'
(Stendahl 1963).

KINSHIP AND MARRIAGE

In 1955 J.K. Campbell, a British anthropologist, spent time doing
field-work with the Sarakatsani, a group of transhumant shep-
herds in the Epirus region of Greece who moved their flocks of
sheep and goats between summer grazing grounds in the moun-
tainous districts of Zagori and winter grazing grounds along the
coast of the Ionian Sea. The work he subsequently published,
entitled *Honour, Family and Patronage* (1964), illustrates many
recurrent features of Mediterranean culture. Seven of the eleven
chapters in Campbell's book deal with kinship and the role of the
family and I will draw on him for particular illustrations of
patterns which are widely evidenced in the writings of other
anthropologists (Pitt-Rivers 1961, 1963 and 1977; Peristiany
1965).

The fundamental division in this society is between kin and
non-kin, between *dikoi* and *xenoi* ('strangers'), with the latter word
being applicable to a non-related family, even if living in the
round hut next door. Fierce competitiveness marks all social
interactions with non-kin, save only when a marriage is to be
arranged, while with kin trust and even altruism are the rule.
Such an outlook is typical of many social groups around the
Mediterranean. The family is a primary seat of group honour.
Affronts to the honour of one member are affronts to the honour
of all. Females are embedded in dominant males, either father,
husband or brother, and must be constantly watched lest they do
anything which might dishonour the family. After all, a man who
seduces a woman wins honour for himself and brings dishonour
on her male relatives. If a sister or daughter willingly loses her
virginity, (her 'shame'), both she and her lover might be killed so
as to repair the profound dishonour such an act brings on the
family. If a sister is raped, her father and brothers are also
dishonoured and vengeance is called for by killing the offender.

Females lead essentially private lives at home. Men lead public
lives. If women go out of the house they may be covered in clothes
from head to foot or even chaperoned to ensure nothing happens
to them which might bring their honour and that of the family
into question. The one activity which regularly takes Mediterranean women outside the house is to fetch water from the well.
Among the Sarakatsani this is regarded as a singularly hazardous
activity as far as the risk to family honour is concerned. A man
intent on seduction need only wait at the well and he will in due

course encounter virtually every woman in the village. The Sarakatsani often require their womenfolk to be chaperoned when getting water, not just to head off actual assault or elopement, but to prevent their neighbours, ever on the look-out for reasons to impugn the family honour, obtaining the slightest pretext for doing so, even if that involves making a false allegation.

Such cultural attitudes help us to interpret the story of Jesus meeting the Samaritan woman at the well in John 4. This is one New Testament passage, in fact, which is difficult to comprehend without attending to such matters, since the conversation between Jesus and the woman reflects the manner in which the respective roles of men and women, especially in the area of sexuality, are defined in terms of honour and shame. In choosing to rest by a well (4.6), Jesus does what a man would do if he was seeking to meet a woman for an illicit purpose. To explain why Jesus acts in such a disreputable way, John mentions that he is weary after the journey and that it is noon, when it was hottest. The text implies that he is thirsty. That is the only possible reason for an honourable man in this social world to wait by a well. Some commentaries explain the reference to the weariness of Jesus as having a theological rationale in that it stresses his humanity, which tends to be overwhelmed in the Fourth Gospel (so Barrett 1978: 231). This explanation is an example of what Bengt Holmberg has aptly called 'the idealistic fallacy', that is, of interpreting phenomena as reflecting theological issues to the neglect of the extent to which ideas are related to social structures (Holmberg 1978). After the disciples have departed, the Samaritan woman comes to draw some water and Jesus, who has no bucket (v.11) and is in genuine need of a drink which she will be able to give him, makes that simple request of her. She is not to know whether he is thirsty or not and as far as she would be aware from her knowledge of why men wait by wells his request might simply be the local equivalent of 'Do you come here often?' In this culture a respectable woman, alone with a man at a well, would ignore the request, or perhaps give the man water in case he was genuinely thirsty, but say nothing to him and leave promptly.

But the Samaritan woman acts shamefully by striking up a conversation. Her reply fixes on the fact that it is strange for a Jew to ask a Samaritan woman for a drink, but the original audience may have understood this to be her way of taking up what might be a pleasant liaison, the local equivalent of 'Why is a nice man like you talking to a girl like me?' The reference later to the fact that she is living with a man not her husband and that she has had five men confirms that she is a woman without honour and corroborates this view. A touch of wry Johannine humour, no doubt meant to underline her shamelessness, emerges a little later when she interprets what Jesus has told her concerning the men in her life as 'Everything I ever did' (v.29). The conversation continues, although in a way which she could hardly have suspected, and when the disciples return they are astounded that Jesus is speaking with a woman (v.27). That they are astonished by this and not by the fact that he is speaking with a Samaritan woman is probably to be understood on the basis that Jesus seems to be acting in the way men bent on dishonour would act and the woman is obviously behaving in a way quite opposite to virtuous. In commenting on this verse C.K. Barrett cites rabbinic warnings against speaking to women in public or at all (Barrett 1978: 240), but the point is far more particular, since wells are places where one's honour may be compromised by accident or design.

A Sarakatsani woman who marries goes off to live with her husband, often in the house he shares with his parents and other siblings. Having spent all their lives sequestered from anyone except close kin, married women are thrown into households where there already exist strong ties between existing members. The lot of the daughter- or sister-in-law is often a very difficult one, at least until she gives birth to her first child, for her sake hopefully a son. Among the Sarakatsani any adult member of such a woman's family-in-law may give her orders, until the birth of her first child. An important feature of such patrilocal marriages is the day on which the bridegroom comes to the house of the woman's family to collect her and take her off to his own home. This event is surrounded with complex rituals. Often there is a great deal of real or ritualised sadness at the bride's home and real or ritualised joy on their return to the bridegroom's. The practice is referred to in the Parable of the Ten Maidens in Matt. 25.1–13. It is unclear in this passage whether the bridegroom is arriving at the bride's house to collect her or returning to his house with her, although the latter is far more likely.

In traditional Mediterranean society marriages are usually arranged, sometimes between kin, as is common in some Arab countries where cousins frequently marry, while in other settings exogamous unions are favoured, as among the Sarakatsani. In either case, however, marriages are a fusion of the honour of both families and even an alliance of their respective commercial interests, since the family tends to be the unit of production. In such a context, where the individual interests of the couple hardly count at all, divorce has a quite different meaning than in modern Western society, since it will involve the possibly acrimonious dissolution of what might have been a socially and economically advantageous union between the two families. The various sayings about divorce in the Synoptic Gospels (Matt. 5.31–2 and 19.1–12; Mark 10.1–12; Luke 16.18) should be understood in this light.

LIMITED GOOD

The broad economic and political environment in which inhabitants of the first-century Mediterranean region lived was divided into agricultural lands worked by people living in villages and small pre-industrial cities populated by a small number of persons, either the local elites or those who tended to their needs. The cities were supported by the surrounding countryside and the strains imposed on the villagers in terms of the amount of produce which they had to supply to the cities were often very great indeed (see Moxnes 1988: 22–74; Oakman 1991; Rohrbaugh 1991). Samuel's warning to the Israelites in 1 Sam. 8.10–18 of what things will be like for them if they have a king nicely encapsulates the burdens thrown upon the agrarian producers by the elites who controlled them in this culture:

> He will take the best of your fields and vineyards and olive orchards and give them to his servants. He will take the tenth of your grain and of your vineyards and give it to his officers and to his servants. He will take your menservants and maidservants, and the best of your cattle and your asses, and put them to his work. He will take the tenth of your flocks, and you shall be his slaves.
>
> (1 Sam. 8.14–17)

Richard Rohrbaugh, who is another member of the Context Group, has recently produced an interpretation of the Lucan Parable of the Great Banquet (Luke 14.15–24) which incisively

employs an understanding of the pre-industrial context to explicate its meaning (Rohrbaugh 1991).

Intrinsic to such a culture, especially the grinding reality of life
for the peasants, was a belief that all goods were limited, both
material and non-material. All goods, from land and food on the
one hand to honour on the other, were regarded as finite in
quantity and always in short supply (Malina 1981: 71–93). The
notion of expanding economies is a very recent one, originating in
the writings of Adam Smith, especially his *Wealth of Nations*,
published in 1776, and of David Ricardo, especially his *Principles
of Political Economy and Taxation*, published in 1817 (see Roll 1973:
154–94). From the Mediterranean perspective, since all goods
were limited, a person could only increase his or her supply of
them at the expense of someone else. Honourable persons,
therefore, worked to preserve what they had, not to accumulate
more. This explains the very negative attitude to trade which one
often observes in this culture. A good example occurs at Eccle-
siasticus 27.2: 'As a stake is driven firmly into a fissure between
stones, so sin is wedged in between selling and buying.'

One way for a member of the non-elite to preserve his position
was to enter into a patron–client relationship with some local
worthy. This was a relationship based on a strong inequality of
power in which, nevertheless, both sides gained, the client by
obtaining social, economic and political resources from the patron, the patron by obtaining useful loyalty and honour.
Patronage is uncommon in Northern European cultures, where it
offends against notions of equality and fair access to resources.
For a modern example, however, we need go no further than the
relations between a Mafia god-father and his 'family'. Sometimes,
middle-men or 'brokers' mediate between patron and client.
Halvor Moxnes has recently interpreted the Lucan account of the
centurion of Caphernaum who sends Jewish elders to Jesus in
terms of a patron using his clients to perform a service for him
(Luke 7.1–10; Moxnes 1991).

CONCLUSION

These cultural patterns provide us, in conclusion, with a set of
models for comprehending the social script in which the New
Testament documents were written, the basic game-rules of this
culture. They equip us with a set of scenarios more appropriate to

the texts than those which we might otherwise employ, often
unconsciously, derived from our very different culture and
experience.

Chapter 3

Glossolalia and the admission of Gentiles into the early Christian community

THE CORNELIUS EPISODE IN ACTS

According to the Acts of the Apostles, the first Gentile to become a Christian was the centurion Cornelius, who was stationed in Caesarea. The story of his conversion, told in the tenth chapter of the work, begins with a brief description of Cornelius, a devout and God-fearing Gentile, already closely aligned with the Jews, who is told in a vision that his prayers have been answered and that he must send someone to Jaffa (a town 30 miles south along the coast) and fetch Peter, then lodging with a tanner. So Cornelius sends off two slaves and a soldier. The next day while they are approaching Jaffa, Peter has a vision of a sheet descending to earth from heaven containing all sorts of animals, some of them unclean, and is told in the vision to kill and eat, which he is unwilling to do, not having before eaten anything unclean. When the emissaries from Cornelius arrive, Peter lets them in, although they are Gentiles, as he has received an instruction to do so from the Spirit in his vision. The next day he sets off with some fellow Jewish Christians to Cornelius. Peter and his group are met in Caesarea by Cornelius and his friends and relatives and are brought into the house of Cornelius. Peter notes that 'It is forbidden (*athemiton*) for Jews to mix with people of another race and visit them, but God has made it clear to me that I must not call anyone profane or unclean' (10.28; The Jerusalem Bible [JB]). A little later Peter delivers an address in which he makes a remarkable leap outside the tight bounds of the Jewish ethnic identity of the time by saying: 'The truth I have now come to realise is that God does not have favourites, but that anybody of any nationality who fears God and does what is right is acceptable to him' (10.34–5; JB). Peter then continues to preach about the life, death and

significance of Jesus and the chapter reaches its climax with the
following passage:

> While Peter was still saying this, the Holy Spirit fell on all who
> heard the word. And the believers from among the circum-
> cised who came with Peter were amazed, because the gift of the
> Holy Spirit had been poured out even on the Gentiles. For they
> heard them speaking in tongues (*lalounton glōssais*) and extoll-
> ing God. Then Peter declared, 'Can any one forbid water for
> baptizing these people who have received the Holy Spirit just as
> we have?' And he commanded them to be baptized in the name
> of Jesus Christ. Then they asked him to remain for some days.
> (10.44–8)

This incident is plainly presented as a second Pentecost akin to the
first Pentecost (recounted in Acts 2.1–11), except that it is a very
much more abbreviated account and contains no express reference to addressing God in foreign tongues. Haenchen correctly
observes that at this point, as at Acts 19.6, the author has in mind
only ecstatic utterance, rather than foreign languages (Haenchen
1971: 354).

It is clear that in this narrative the pouring out of the Holy
Spirit upon the Gentiles, manifested in glossolalia, serves as the
final and irrefutable legitimation for the acceptance of the Gentiles into the community. The fact that Peter can ask in Acts 10.47
whether anyone could refuse baptism to such people, now that
they had received the Holy Spirit, raises the possibility that
without the gift of the Holy Spirit some might doubt whether
baptism was appropriate. Accordingly, the author presents the
manifestation of the gifts of the Holy Spirit, especially glossolalia,
as the critical factor in the acceptance of Gentiles into the Christian community, which acceptance extends ultimately to their
being welcomed into eucharistic table-fellowship with Jewish
members of the community.

The question which remains, however, is whether the importance of glossolalia in the admission of Gentiles into the early
Christian communities is merely a Lucan theme or whether it also
accords with the historical reality of the Christian movement in its
earliest period. This, of course, raises the difficult question of the
extent to which one may expect historical accuracy from the Acts
of the Apostles. Late in the nineteenth century a view gained
currency among British New Testament scholars that if the

author of Acts was accurate in some details, especially of broad historical setting, it was reasonable to suppose that he would prove accurate where his accuracy could not be checked, in particular, of course, with respect to the manner in which he had crafted his narrative. This conclusion, which has been energetically supported in our own time by F.F. Bruce and his followers, such as W.W. Gasque (1975), is of dubious worth. It is falsified by the phenomenon of the carefully researched historical novel, which is still a novel even though its author may have got the details of its setting right. Although Acts is not a novel, the analogy holds. We must always consider how the author may have recast sources and traditions at his disposal in the light of his own particular purpose and weigh the consequences of such activity for the historical reliability of the work. When one turns to the Cornelius episode, in particular, it is clear that the difficulties in the way of defending the historicity of the narrative as related by Luke are so great and have been so meticulously exposed by German scholarship in particular, that the persistence into the present of a belief in its historicity is a cause for wonder. The principal objection to the narrative, as I have noted elsewhere (1987: 95–6), is not that it is so heavily mythological, although that is no small objection to its historicity, but that it is wildly inconsistent both with later parts of Acts (especially Acts 15) and with the subsequent antipathy of Peter (and James behind him) to Jewish–Gentile table-fellowship in Antioch (Gal. 2.11–14).

The fact that the narrative may not, as it is presented by Luke, accord with historical fact does not, however, mean that it may not contain a core of historical truth, possibly even a core of great significance in our understanding of early Christianity. I have elsewhere argued that the admission of Gentiles into early Christian communities may have begun as early as the first communities in Jerusalem, possibly as a result of Greek-speaking Jewish Christians such as Stephen responding to the acute sense of marginalisation experienced by their God-fearing Gentile friends in Jerusalem by virtue of their being excluded from the Temple cult (1987: 154–9). My aim in this chapter is to move beyond such factors to consider whether the account of the conversion of Cornelius actually reveals the precise reason for the admission of Gentiles and their complete acceptance into the early Christian communities.

In considering the significance of glossolalia I propose to use for comparative purposes material produced by modern anthropological, ethnographic and psychological studies of glossolalia and related phenomena in contemporary religious settings. One must observe the usual methodological caution in employing social-scientific ideas and approaches with respect to New Testament material, but as Gerd Theissen has noted, although the results of modern research 'cannot serve as support for historical theses, they can serve as a heuristic starting point and as illustration' (Theissen 1987: 269). This is not to deny, of course, as he notes in one context, but in a way which has a wider relevance, that 'Hypotheses about glossolalia in Corinth can originate from observation of contemporary phenomena, but they must be verified exclusively on the basis of the historical sources' (Theissen 1987: 269).

MODERN RESEARCH INTO GLOSSOLALIA

There is now a considerable body of research into contemporary manifestations of glossolalia and related charismatic phenomena, most helpfully in the writings of W.J. Samarin, J.P. Kildahl and F.D. Goodman. Perhaps the most useful work for comparison with the New Testament data is that by Felicitas D. Goodman in the area of social psychology entitled *Speaking in Tongues: A Cross-Cultural Study of Glossolalia* (1972). Goodman's investigation into the phenomena involved the analysis of tape recordings made by other researchers during the services of a number of religious groups, such as the Streams of Power movement of the Caribbean island of St Vincent, a midwestern tent revival in Colombus, Ohio, the Umbanda spiritualist cult in Brazil and mainline Protestant churches in Texas, together with her own lengthy participant observation and recording (on tape and film) of dissociative states and glossolalia among a Spanish-speaking Pentecostal congregation in Mexico City and a Mayan-speaking branch of the same church in Yucatan. Goodman was able to demonstrate the existence of features of dissociative states and glossolalia common to all of the groups she studied, in spite of the differences in language, culture and even religion (the Umbanda cult being non-Christian).

It is appropriate to offer a brief summary of the main results of Goodman's research:

1   Although among some of the groups which Goodman surveyed was a belief that glossolalia was actually speech in a
foreign tongue, that is, an ordinary human language that
could be understood if someone who knew that language
happened to be present, a phenomenon known as
xenoglossy, it is highly unlikely that this ever occurs. She
concluded that glossolalia never consists of another language
unknown to the speaker; glossolalia is 'lexically non-
communicative'. The person uttering the glossolalia and his
or her listeners do not and could not share a linguistic code.
'Glossolalia', she writes, quoting T. Spoerri, 'involves . . . the
privation of the informative and communicative side of
discourse, speech becomes musical sound' (1972: 123).

2   Her investigations revealed important agreements in the
glossolalia utterance across seven cultural settings and four
different languages. Thus, she found that glossolalia was
uttered in pulses, with each pulse beginning with a consonant and ending with a vowel. The pulses exhibited an
accentual system using stress, with a primary and secondary
accent. Within each utterance unit was an intonation pattern
regularly showing an onset in the medium range, a peak and
a sloping gradient leading to an often precipitous decay
(121–2).

3   One of her principal findings was that the subjects of her
investigation only broke into glossolalia when in a state of
'dissociation', that is, when they had withdrawn as it were into
an inner space, and had dissociated themselves from the
everyday realities surrounding them. In other words, they
had entered an 'altered state of consciousness', to use a more
scientific description, or, in more traditional and far less
exact language, they were in the grip of hysteria, frenzy,
ecstasy or madness. Some other writers, including W.J.
Samarin, have doubted that glossolalia always occurs in the
context of dissociation, but this was certainly the case with
respect to the communities studied by Goodman.

4   The dissociative state in which glossolalia occurs may also be
the context for other phenomena, such as unusual kinetic
movements, like shaking, catatonic-like states and hallucinations, both auditory and visual. On one occasion (she was
more careful thereafter) Goodman herself involuntarily

went into a state of dissociation, during which she had a powerful vision of light.

5   Many of the persons studied by Goodman experienced a feeling of peace, even euphoria, at the conclusion of the dissociative state.

6   The recipients of glossolalia generally regarded it as a manifestation of the Holy Spirit. Goodman's reaction to the first occasion upon which she witnessed glossolalia indicates the naturalness of this interpretation:

> I can easily see now why glossolalia is so universally considered a divine inspiration, a possession by a supernatural being. There is something incredibly, brutally elemental about such an outbreak of vocalisation, and at the same time something eerily, frighteningly unreal.
>
> (15)

7   The fact that glossolalia is interpreted as the manifestation of the Holy Spirit inevitably results in its being a matter of prestige for those members of the community who have exhibited it (89). Conversely, a person who had been a member of a congregation for some time without producing glossolalia might be criticised on the basis that he or she was too sinful to receive it.

8   In general glossolalia and related phenomena are learned within the context of a particular group through the facilitation of their leader. Goodman cites a number of cases of evangelists who are already capable of powerfully manifesting glossolalia going to a new congregation and causing outbreaks of dissociative states and glossolalia where before these phenomena had been non-existent or only manifested by some of the members. Interesting confirmation that people can be taught dissociation and glossolalia by their leader arises from the fact that the utterances of the rank and file of the group, which quickly become stereotyped, mirror that of the person who guided the glossolalists into the behaviour. She notes that 'there is little variation of sound pattern within the group arising around a particular guide' (123).

9   One of the most remarkable of her observations is the phenomenon of spontaneous glossolalia which occurs without the person concerned ever having witnessed it before (70). She relates that on one occasion in Yucatan 'a boy

wandered into the church and, upon seeing some *hermanos* (i.e. male members of the congregation) going into glossolalia, also dissociated and produced a vocalisation. He never came back to the church.' Given that glossolalia is usually seen as a manifestation of the Holy Spirit, its appearance in someone who may be a complete non-believer inevitably prompts some theological explanation to make sense of the occurrence.

10   Among the groups she studied, Goodman noted a great anxiety if a person spoke in tongues who had not yet been baptised by immersion. She explains the reason for this as follows:

> Such persons, although 'very close to God' are in grave ritual danger, from which only water baptism can save them. The anthropologist is familiar with this kind of anxiety attendant upon contact with what is thought to be divine in the belief systems of many societies.
>
> (87)

11   Goodman noted that there was a tendency for glossolalia to fade over time. Within the period of two or so years covered by her observations in Mexico City and Yucatan she noticed that there occurred a considerable decline in the energy discharged during the utterances, which was manifested in a decrease in loudness, intensity and pitch between the lowest and highest points of the utterance, as well as in the disappearance of the majority of high-effort vowels (i, u) (95–6).

GLOSSOLALIA AND DISSOCIATIVE STATES AMONG THE CHRISTIAN COMMUNITY AT CORINTH

As already noted, the aim of this chapter is to determine whether the manifestation of glossolalia by Gentiles might have been the factor which overcame Jewish opposition to their becoming full members of early Christian communities. It is, accordingly, necessary to consider the phenomenon of glossolalia in the earliest Christian communities to which we have access in the light of the modern materials just considered. When it comes to comparing these contemporary analogies with the New Testament data, the most appropriate place with which to begin is not the Pentecost narrative in Acts 2 (at first blush, perhaps, the most likely candidate because of its place at the beginning of the Christian story), but Paul's treatment in 1 Corinthians 12–14. The reason for this is that in Paul we have an eye-witness to glossolalia and other features associated with the onset of the Holy Spirit from first-generation Christianity, whereas the author of Acts was writing much later, probably in the period 80–95 CE, and may or may not (an issue taken up later) have personally encountered these phenomena. The very different quality of the evidence offered by Paul and Luke on this subject has been insufficiently appreciated by some commentators (see the writings of S.D. Currie and W.G. MacDonald in Mills 1986).

In carrying out the comparison, while always mindful of Theissen's warning that the results of modern social-scientific research cannot serve as proof for historical theses, we must be open to the prospect that we may be able to conclude as a matter of probability (and historical research is always a matter of probabilities) that in Paul's Corinth we are dealing with the same phenomenon as that observed by Goodman, or at least a similar one. In any event, even if this conclusion cannot eventually be drawn, the very process of undertaking the comparison will constitute an exercise in sociological imagination which is likely to produce a new agenda of exegetical questions which are rooted in the actual religious experience of real communities, rather than originating in a scholarship imbued with the rationalist attitudes of the university or seminary.

The feature of primary significance in Paul's treatment of glossolalia in 1 Corinthians is his repeated assertion and assumption of its unintelligibility to those present, including those responsible for producing it. The clearest expression of this is found at 14.2: 'For the one who speaks in a tongue (lalōn glōsse) speaks not to men but to God; for no one understands him, but he utters mysteries in the Spirit.' A little later he notes that glossolalia is not intelligible utterance (mē eusēmos logos) (14.9). Another statement as to the unintelligibility of glossolalia is found at 14.16. Furthermore, it is clear from 14.13–14 that even a glossolalist himself may not be able to understand his utterance. In the absence of interpretation, glossolalia is unintelligible, it is 'speaking in the air' (14.9).

Glossolalia does not mean 'speaking in a foreign tongue' for Paul. This is corroborated by the reference to foreign languages (heteroglōssoi) in the loose quotation from Isa. 28.11–12 in 1 Cor.

14.21. Here Paul is using foreign languages as an analogy for glossolalia – 'A redundant exercise if, in fact, the Corinthians were indeed speaking foreign languages' (Williams 1981: 31). It is essential to bear in mind how odd the use of *glōssa* in the sense of a 'language' or 'dialect' without an epithet meaning 'foreign' (such as *heteros* or *allos*) or referring to a particular nationality (Athenian, Roman or barbarian, for example) would have seemed to a first-century CE speaker of Greek. Glossolalia may well be a Christian neologism. It is not mentioned, for example, by the second-century CE writer Julius Pollux in his extensive list of words relating to divine possession and prophecy (*Onomastikon* 1.15–19). Paul does not explain exactly what he means by interpretation, although it must consist of a member of the community with that gift listening to the glossolalia and proffering an intelligible message in its stead. At 1 Cor. 12.10 interpretation is presented as one of the spiritual gifts; it is something which can be prayed for (1 Cor. 14.13). It cannot mean the ability to translate a foreign language which one obtains through instruction and practice.

Accordingly, it is necessary to dissent from the view proffered by Christopher Forbes in a recent Macquarie University doctoral thesis that in 1 Corinthians Paul is actually speaking of xenoglossy and not glossolalia (1987). Other scholars have also expressed such a view (Davies 1952, for example). The glossolalia described by Paul as present in the Corinthian community is, therefore, similar to that among the contemporary congregations considered above in being 'lexically non-communicative'. The widespread fiction that the phenomenon is explicable as speech in human languages unknown to the speaker is entirely absent from Paul's account. Paul's presentation of glossolalia as unintelligible utterance rather than xenoglossy vouches for his dispassionate accuracy on this topic and lays the foundation for establishing the comparability of the Corinthian position with the findings from modern research.

There are some features in 1 Cor. 12–14 which suggest that the context for the glossolalia occurring in the community was a state of dissociation which Goodman argues always accompanies modern examples of the phenomenon. At one point, Paul states that if he engages in glossolalia prayer, his spirit prays, but his mind is fruitless (*ho de nous mou akarpos estin*) (14.14). This unusual expression may refer to the disengagement of the consciousness from everyday reality. Another possible indication of altered states of consciousness can be found in 1 Cor. 14.23: 'If, therefore, the whole church assembles and all speak in tongues, and outsiders (*idiōtai*) or unbelievers (*apistoi*) enter, will they not say that you are mad.'

The word for 'you are mad' (*mainesthai*) had, prior to its use here, long been used with respect to outbreaks of religious madness (*mania*), that is to say, dissociative states occurring in the context of religious expression. The word may have that meaning here (Conzelmann 1975: 243). On the other hand, this interpretation may place inadequate stress on the fact that the words 'you are mad' constitute a potential response by an outsider to a situation where all of the community are engaging in glossolalia. Thus, Paul may not be relating *mania* (ritual madness) to glossolalia itself, but to the wild scenes of chaos and disorder when all present indulge in it, even if they do not, as individuals, lapse into a trance. For this reason, it cannot be said that this verse itself offers unambiguous evidence for dissociative states attending glossolalia at Corinth, although that interpretation remains an intriguing possibility. More interesting, perhaps, are the verses immediately following (14.24–5) which proclaim that if an unbeliever (*apistos*) or outsider (*idiōtēs*) enters the community when everyone is prophesying, a process which involves intelligible statements (cf. 14.3–6), the secrets of his heart will be disclosed and he will declare, 'Truly, God is among you.' It appears that underlying Paul's argument at this point is a claim by the Corinthians that God is among them in glossolalia, which claim Paul, without denying its validity, adjusts by emphasising that God would be seen as present in general prophesying by the community. Since the idea that religious trances and ecstasy were the manifestation of possession by a god was one of wide currency in Greek and Near Eastern religions in Paul's day, it is likely that a claim by the Corinthians that God was in them or among them during glossolalia meant that the phenomenon was occurring during states of dissociation.

This section of 1 Corinthians does not contain references to other charismatic phenomena which often accompany glossolalia, such as unusual movements and hallucinations, auditory and visual. However, we know from other evidence that Paul himself was, indeed, the recipient of visions (cf. 1 Cor. 9.1; 2 Cor. 12.1–7).

There is abundant evidence for the fact that Paul's Corinthian converts saw glossolalia as a manifestation of the Holy Spirit. The problem was that they placed too much emphasis on it. This explains Paul's attempt to arrange the various gifts in hierarchical order with glossolalia and its interpretation at the bottom (12.28–31). Since it would appear from 1 Cor. 14.5 that Paul was faced with the situation at Corinth where not everyone manifested glossolalia, and where those who did obviously treated it as a very high, if not the highest, spiritual gift, it follows that to have manifested the Holy Spirit in this way was a matter of some prestige in the community.

In terms of Mediterranean shame–honour culture, there is disagreement whether the manifestation of glossolalia was a sign of ascribed or acquired honour, that is, of honour one was given, or did something to acquire. As J. Neyrey has argued, Paul's insistence that the charismatic phenomena are divine gifts (1 Cor. 1.4–5, 12.4–11) means that they constitute ascribed honour from his perspective. But it appears that some members of the community boasted as if these features were the products of their own achievement (1 Cor. 4.7); in other words, that they are an honour they have acquired on their own (Neyrey 1990). Paul says nothing about those who do not engage in glossolalia, but one may surmise that they were regarded as inferior in honour and status, perhaps on modern analogies even sinful, by those members of the community who did. Such antipathy was, of course, inimical to the unity of the congregation which Paul so earnestly strove to establish.

Another area in which the Pauline data can be compared with modern material is in the manner in which glossolalia and other manifestations of the Spirit were initiated among the Corinthians. We know that Paul himself founded this community (1 Cor. 3.6, 3.10) and that his initial preaching at Corinth was expressed in a 'demonstration of spirit and of power (*dunamis*)' (1 Cor. 2.4). Thus, Paul insists upon his own credentials as gifted by the Holy Spirit near the beginning of the letter. He must be referring here to his having demonstrated the various gifts of the Spirit which he lists later (12.8–10), including, as we gather from the word *dunamis*, the working of miracles (cf. 12.10). Even more interesting than this, however, is his categorical assertion 'I thank God that I speak in tongues more than all of you' (14.18). Putting these two

statements together, then, we obtain a picture of Paul as powerfully manifesting the Holy Spirit in preaching, miracle-working
and glossolalia. We may confidently assume (Conzelmann 1975:
204) that it was Paul who kindled the expression of spiritual gifts
among the Corinthian community. Indeed, to adopt Max Weber's
model of the charismatic leader and his followers, it is possible
that it was by the very fact of demonstrating his extraordinary
powers in the areas of miracle-working and glossolalia, and facilit-
ating those powers among them, that Paul won the Corinthians to
the Gospel and established the community (Gerth and Mills1970:
245–52). In all of this there are striking similarities to the modern
Pentecostal evangelists described by Goodman, who are able to
produce strong glossolalia and to ignite outbreaks of the phenomenon among the congregations to which they are sent. From
the modern parallels, it is possible that the glossolalia produced
by Paul's Corinthians closely mirrored his own.

1 Corinthians is silent on the attitude which Paul and his
followers would have held towards a person who manifested
glossolalia prior to baptism. However, it is clear that the usual
order was for the gifts of the Holy Spirit to be given after baptism
(1 Cor. 12.13). Accordingly, it may well be the case that if a non-
baptised outsider were to exhibit glossolalia at a meeting of the
community there would be a view in favour of bringing an end to
this anomaly by baptising the person, assuming he or she were so
willing.

Interesting confirmation of the strength of the ecstatic powers
unleashed in Corinth subsists in the fact that the glossolalia there
does not appear to have been subject to the attenuation noticed by
Goodman among contemporary movements. Paul does, of
course, note that, unlike love, glossolalia along with knowledge
and prophecy will be destroyed (13.8). But he is only referring to
its (and their) destruction at the *eschaton* – or as he says, 'when
perfection comes' (13.10). So although Paul emphasises the provi-
sional nature of the spiritual gifts from the perspective of the End,
he gives no indication of their diminution in the meantime. Yet,
since it is indisputable that glossolalia (and perhaps some of the
other gifts) did eventually die out in the early church, Goodman's
views on its attenuation over time are thereby confirmed. We do,
however, appear to be looking at a longer time-scale for achieving
this result than that observed by her. It would appear that by the
time the Pastoral Epistles were written later in the first century,

much of the ecstatic excitement of the earlier period had sub-
sided. The question arises from this whether Luke, who was
writing in the 80s or 90s of the first century, had personally
experienced glossolalia. For reasons explained a little below, his
presentation of what happened at Pentecost does not encourage
confidence in this phenomenon having been current among the
group or groups for whom he was writing.

GLOSSOLALIA AND THE MEANING OF PENTECOST

Glossolalia of the type present among the followers of Jesus in
Corinth must have had a beginning at some point in the development of the first communities. Moreover, although there are
parallels for different forms of ecstatic utterance by specialist
individuals such as shamans and medicine men, glossolalia by
groups of lay persons is extremely rare. As L. Carlyle May noted in
a 1956 world survey of glossolalia and related phenomena in
contemporary non-Christian religions, there were no examples to
be found outside of the Christian context of whole groups of
worshippers being motivated by a few practising glossolalists to
utter strange sounds. Moreover, Christopher Forbes has per-
suasively argued that it is extremely difficult to find any parallels
whatsoever for early Christian glossolalia within the traditions of
Graeco-Roman religion (1987). This means, of course, that Christian glossolalia and related phenomena such as states of
dissociation almost certainly stood out as highly unusual in the
first-century urban environment and must have exercised a potent attraction upon those who came in contact with them.

According to Acts 2.1–13, the gifts of the Holy Spirit were first
poured out at the feast of Pentecost after the death and resurrection of Jesus. Luke relates how this occurrence began with
auditory and visual phenomena and climaxed in the Jewish
disciples of Jesus who were present speaking in foreign tongues
which they had apparently not previously learned. Luke is portraying xenoglossy, not glossolalia. Nevertheless, using Paul's
experience as a control against which to measure this passage and
given the widespread error of interpreting glossolalia as
xenoglossy, especially perhaps by people not personally ac-
quainted with glossolalia, we may be reasonably confident that
Luke is in error here. In all probability, the earliest outbreak of
'tongues' took the form of glossolalia and not xenoglossy. Luke

may well be relying on earlier traditions which have become distorted over time as glossolalia died out among the Christian communities and the nature of the phenomenon became misunderstood in the absence of first-hand experience of it. But there seems little reason to doubt that the first outbreak of glossolalia involved only Jewish disciples and occurred very early in the history of the Christian movement, quite possibly among the first Aramaic-speaking community in Jerusalem. When one takes into account the overwhelming impression made upon those who experience dissociative states which are interpreted as possession by the Holy Spirit and the rarity, perhaps even uniqueness, of such experiences among urban religious groups of this period, the Pentecost event may well have triggered the enthusiastic spread of the Christian message just as Luke described. Nor indeed should we doubt that auditory and visual phenomena akin to those reported in Acts 2.2–3 accompanied the onset of glossolalia at this time.

GLOSSOLALIA AND THE ADMISSION OF THE GENTILES

We are now in a position to assess the likelihood of Acts 10.44–48 expressing a fundamental fact of the dawn of Christian history – the explanation for the admission of Gentiles to the early communities – even if the particular dramatic setting provided in Acts for that explanation is a development by Luke or the tradition before him. It is beyond doubt that in some places at least Gentiles were allowed into Christian communities even if initially only with the status of observers and not members. The best evidence for this is the fact that Paul's Corinthian congregation was in the habit of permitting unbelievers (*apistoi*) and outsiders (*idiōtai*) to be present, even while glossolalia was occurring (1 Cor. 14.24). My own research elsewhere provides support for the presence of Gentiles even among the original communities in Jerusalem (1987: 154–63). Once we have Gentiles present while Jews engaged in glossolalia, the contemporary material surveyed by Goodman suggests that such outsiders may themselves have broken into ecstatic utterance, just indeed as Saul, upon meeting a group of prophets in ecstasy on their way down from a high place near Gibeah, himself fell into ecstasy and began to prophesy (1 Sam. 10.5–12). Dissociative states are contagious. Once this had happened, the fact that such an event was interpreted as possession by the Holy Spirit, together perhaps with some ritual unease that a non-baptised person had been touched by God, would have constituted the strongest imaginable inducement for the existing Jewish members of the congregation to abandon their deep-seated aversion to mingling with Gentiles which was necessary for the protection of a Jewish ethnos in a Gentile world (see Esler 1987: 73–86). This meant allowing them to be initiated into the community by baptism and to share in its full life thereafter, even to the extent of engaging with them in the eucharistic table-fellowship of the one loaf and the one cup. This is exactly what Luke describes as happening in Acts 10.44–8. The accuracy of his description of this process is even reflected in the detail that, as noted above, he has glossolalia in mind here and not the xenoglossy which features in his account of the first Pentecost.

Accordingly, we conclude that Acts 10.44–8 is historically accurate in revealing a fact of fundamental importance for the beginnings of Christianity – that the admission of Gentiles into the early communities was the result of their manifesting glossolalia and other gifts of the Holy Spirit at meetings of existing Jewish congregations.

Chapter 4

Sectarianism and the conflict at Antioch

THE ISSUE

In Chapter 1 I outlined a model of the sectarianism involved in a group separating from an existing church and employed it to pose a number of questions regarding the beginnings of the early Christian communities in Jerusalem. An essential feature of the model was the issue of whether such a depth of division had been reached between the parent church and the new religious movement that joint membership of both was no longer possible. Only at this point was it appropriate to call the new body a 'sect'. I also suggested that in the context of first-century Judaism one indication of whether a breaking-point of this kind had been reached was whether a particular Christian community practised Jewish–Gentile table-fellowship, especially eucharistic table-fellowship, where those present shared, that is to say, actually passed around from hand to hand, one loaf of bread and one cup of wine, in the manner and with the significance described by Paul:

> The cup of blessing which we bless, is it not a participation in the blood of Christ? The bread which we break, is it not a participation in the body of Christ? Because there is one bread, we who are many are one body; for we all partake of the one bread.

> (1 Cor. 10.16–17)

Although there was nothing to stop the members of his congregations engaging in ordinary meals, this form of table-fellowship, where the one loaf and the one cup symbolised, or rather enacted, the oneness of the community in Christ, was the one which mattered to Paul. Other meals could be eaten at home. Paul at one point rebukes the Corinthians in these terms:

When you meet together, it is not the Lord's supper (*kuriakon deipnon*) that you eat. For in eating, each one goes ahead with his own meal, and one is hungry and another is drunk. What! do you not have houses to eat and drink in? Or do you despise the church of God and humiliate those who have nothing? What shall I say to you? Shall I commend you in this ? No, I will not.

(1 Cor.11.20–2)

The eucharistic meal was the most tangible expression of the unity in Jesus Christ of Jew and Gentile, slave and free, male and female which he valued so highly (Gal. 3.28). The Lord's Supper (*kuriakon deipnon*) was integral to the very existence and life of his communities.

I have elsewhere explored the question of table-fellowship in Luke–Acts, and certain social-scientific perspectives relevant to it, and I do not intend repeating that discussion here (1987: 71–109). My aim in this chapter is to focus upon the conflict at Antioch between Paul and Peter (with Barnabas and the other Jewish Christians behind him) as described by Paul in the second chapter of his letter to the Galatians. I will argue that Paul's position on mixed table-fellowship reveals that the form of Christianity he advocated for communities containing Jewish and Gentile Christians was sectarian (in the sense referred to above) with respect to Judaism. This discussion will require some coverage of two aspects of my views on table-fellowship which have drawn criticism from some quarters, namely, whether there actually was a prohibition of some sort upon Jews in the first century dining with Gentiles and whether the dispute at Antioch reported by Paul in the second chapter of Galatians is related to such a prohibition or is to be explained on some other basis. I will begin with the broad context in Galatians in which the account of the incident at Antioch is set.

THE GALATIAN CONTEXT

Paul despatched his letter to the Galatians, probably in the early to mid-50s of the first-century CE (Betz 1979: 11–12), to deal with a particular problem which had arisen among certain communities he had founded in what is now Turkey. Broadly speaking, the problem arose because after Paul had left the area certain people had begun exerting pressure upon the Gentile members of the

Galatian communities to be circumcised and to take on the obligations of the Jewish Law. Paul is infuriated by this development. He even expresses a wish that the trouble-makers would castrate themselves (5.12). The fundamental basis of Paul's attitude is almost certainly a theological one: he and the Galatians know that Christ is the source of righteousness, as manifested most dramatically in the gifts of the Holy Spirit (3.2–5), and that this fact simply leaves no room for any other agent of redemption: 'For if justification were through the law, then Christ died to no purpose' (Gal. 2.21).

Paul had founded the Galatian communities (1.6). He describes what he had given them as 'the Gospel of Christ' (1.7). His initial way of stating the difficulty which has arisen is that they are so quickly deserting him who called them in favour of 'a different Gospel' (*heteron euaggelion* – 1.6). Then he immediately corrects himself by saying that there is no 'other [Gospel]', but rather there are some who are disturbing (*tarassontes*) the Galatians and seeking to overturn the Gospel of Christ (1.7). One gathers both from this correction and from 1.8 that whoever the 'disturbers' might be, they are claiming the word 'Gospel' as appropriate to their version of the movement. Paul's strong antipathy to any other Gospel is expressed in his wish that its proponents be accursed (1.9). At issue between Paul and his rivals in Galatia is something going to the very nature of gospel.

It is quite clear that whatever the precise meaning of this 'different Gospel', those who are propounding it are actively seeking to have the Gentile members of the communities circumcised. There are three passages where this becomes apparent, at 5.2–3, 5.12 and 6.12–13. The first of these is particularly revealing: 'Now I, Paul, say to you that if you receive circumcision, Christ will be of no advantage to you. I testify again to every man who receives circumcision that he is bound to keep the whole law.' Circumcision of Gentiles was certainly not an aspect of the Gospel Paul had originally preached, but it is associated with or a facet of the different Gospel to which the Galatians are now being exposed. The text offers some data suggesting that he knew something as to the motivation and attitudes of his opponents, but perhaps without being aware of their identity. Thus he describes them as the ones who are disturbing the Galatians and overturning the Gospel of Christ (1.7) and later refers to 'he who is disturbing you . . . whoever he is' (5.10). Possibly, this may mean that Paul did know the identity of at least one of the trouble-makers, but did not wish to name him. There is an interesting, albeit cryptic, description of their behaviour at 4.17, to which I will return below: 'They pay zealous court to you not in a good way, but they intend to exclude you (*ekkleisai*), in order that you court them' (Betz 1979: 220).

The most illuminating passage as to the nature of Paul's opponents occurs near the end of the letter where Paul adds a message in his own hand:

> It is those people who wish to make a nice appearance in the flesh that compel you to be circumcised – only so that they may not be persecuted for the cross of Christ. For not even the circumcised themselves keep the Law, but they want you to be circumcised, in order that they may boast in your flesh.
>
> (6.12–14; Betz 1979: 312)

This passage suggests that the cross of Christ itself is not a cause of persecution, since if those seeking circumcision of the Gentiles are successful they will not be persecuted. One assumes, more-over, that by 'cross of Christ' Paul is making some generalised reference to the Christian message and lifestyle. Accordingly, for Paul's opponents being a Christian itself is not a problem. What is problematic for them is allowing the Gentile members of the communities to be uncircumcised. Some aspect of the life of the communities, apart from their central faith in Christ, is so serious an issue that it is leading to persecution of some of the members and can only be rectified by circumcision of the Gentiles. Now it might have been the case that Paul's opponents were motivated by nobler motives than he imputes to them. But even if that were so, it would still be necessary, for Paul's letter to have any effect, that the type of motivation he attributes to them was a possible one in the circumstances.

Who were the persecutors and who the persecuted? It is impossible within the ambit of this work to summarise the long history of scholarship on this matter (for which see Howard 1979) or to present a thoroughly detailed proposal of my own; only a brief sketch is possible. Although occasionally suggested, it can hardly be the case that Gentiles are doing the persecuting, since what interest would they have in circumcision? There are really only three possibilities, either Jews *simpliciter* or Jewish Christians or a coalition of both. This a very difficult question. Bearing in

mind, however, that the persecution envisaged in Gal. 6.12 must
have involved the use of a certain degree of force, it is probable
that there was some involvement by the local Jewish authorities,
since the synagogue could order beatings and possibly imprison-
ment (cf. 2 Cor. 11.23–30). Purely Jewish Christian activity seems
unlikely. But it is not impossible to imagine Jewish Christians
either encouraging the local synagogue authorities to act or co-
operating with them when they did. As to the identity of those
who are under pressure to encourage Gentiles to be circumcised
to avoid persecution, these can only be Jewish Christians. Local
Gentiles were not subject to Jewish discipline or persecution.

We are now in a position to propose a scenario which accounts
for the data one may draw or deduce from Paul as to what was
going on in Galatia. If one were to play the Devil's advocate and to
assume that in the particular localities in which the Galatian
communities were situated there were uncircumcised Gentile
Christians and circumcised Jewish Christians having no contact
with them, how could there have been any pressure upon local
Jewish Christians to ensure that these Gentiles became circumcised? The Gentiles would simply have been of no concern of
theirs and they could hardly have been held responsible for them.
Why would the Jewish members of the congregations suffer
persecution on account of the activities of Gentiles whom they
might not even have known and over whom they would presumably have had no influence? Asking these questions brings home
the fact that the issue at stake in Galatia only makes sense if there is
some nexus between the Jewish Christians being persecuted and
the Gentile Christians whom they must get circumcised to avoid
being persecuted. There must be a sufficient degree of intercon-
nection between them to make realistic a situation in which the
uncircumcised status of the Gentiles is both a cause of great
offence to wider Jewish opinion and also regarded as a problem
which the Jewish Christians are in a position to do something
about. The only context which satisfies these requirements is a
Christian community of which both Jewish Christians and Gentiles are members.

Yet if this is the only context which makes sense of the pressures on Paul's opponents to have the Gentiles circumcised and to
do so purportedly pursuant to what they claimed was the Gospel,
we have still not isolated the precise nature of the offence which so
concerned Jewish opinion and which could only be solved by

circumcision of the Gentile members of mixed Jewish–Gentile Christian communities. The answer to this question depends upon reading the letter as a totality and in the light of other information we have as to the nature of Jewish–Gentile relationships in the first-century, but for the moment we will make two observations. First, whatever the nature of the problem as perceived by Paul's opponents in Galatia, only the drastic action of circumcision would suffice as its remedy. In other words, only if the Gentile Christians became Jews could the affront to Jewish sentiment caused by their association with Jewish Christians be ended. Secondly, the admittedly elliptic verse 4.17, quoted above, may throw light on the subject, in its reference to the intention of Paul's rivals being 'to exclude' his addressees. This seems to refer to a desire to 'shut out' the Gentile Christians, in other words, to break off association with them. It is possible that the word *ekkleisai* conjures up the same activity as that described in 2.12–13, where Peter, Barnabas and the rest of the Jews in Antioch broke off their previous association, including table-fellowship, with the Gentile members. If so, might it not be the case that the same matter was at issue in Galatia as had previously vexed the church in Antioch? If so, it would follow that at Antioch (as was later to be the case in Galatia) the problem was one so serious that only circumcision of the Gentiles could provide the answer. This is a factor which must be borne in mind in seeking to isolate the relationship between the autobiographical passage and the rest of the letter and the precise nature of the problem at Antioch.

THE CONNECTION BETWEEN THE ANTIOCHEAN AND GALATIAN CONTEXTS

A striking feature of Galatians is that Paul spends a fair proportion of it (27 verses out of 149) on an autobiographical passage describing how he became an apostle, after having persecuted the church, his early dealings with the apostles in Jerusalem and the important agreement he subsequently reached with them to the effect that he would carry the Gospel to the Gentiles just as they carried it to the Jews, and the incident at Antioch (1.12–2.14). Paul's actual account of the conflict at Antioch occupies only four verses of the letter:

> But when Cephas came to Antioch I opposed him to his face, because he stood condemned. For before certain men came

from James, he ate with the Gentiles; but when they came he drew back and separated himself, fearing the circumcision party. And with him the rest of the Jews acted insincerely, so that even Barnabas was carried away by their insincerity. But when I saw they were not being straightforward about the truth of the gospel, I said to Cephas before them all, 'If you, though a Jew, live like a Gentile and not like a Jew, how can you compel the Gentiles to live like Jews?'

(2.11–14)

Unlike some critics (Dunn 1990: 158 and 172; Verseput 1993: 51), I do not consider that vv.15–21 form part of what Paul said to Peter at Antioch. Paul inserts the autobiographical material in 1.12–2.14 into a letter which he writes some time later to his Galatian addressees presumably because it bears upon the particular difficulties they are encountering. The fact that he does this must surely be a critical issue in seeking to interpret the precise nature of the Antioch incident. For this reason, although the particular nature of the relationship between the two situations remains to be considered, the most attractive exegetical path is to investigate the situation in Galatia which has led Paul to write this letter to them and to use the results of that investigation as a guide to the meaning of the events in Antioch.

It is unfortunate that Professor J.D.G. Dunn, the author of an important article on the subject (1983 and 1990), has sought to interpret the Antioch incident without detailed reference to the wider Galatian issue, which he only mentions at the end of his discussion as apparently confirming his views (1990: 161–2). In this latter regard Dunn's approach is at least preferable to that of E.P. Sanders, who has recently joined the discussion on this topic and attempted to explicate the meaning of Gal. 2.11–14 by employing his justly renowned grasp on the Jewish material but without any reference whatever to the immediate Galatian context of Paul's account of events at Antioch (Sanders 1990).

The developing research into the bearing of Greek and Roman rhetoric on the New Testament, associated especially with H.D. Betz (1975 and 1979) and G.A. Kennedy (1984), is relevant in determining how the autobiographical passage in Gal. 1.12–2.14 is related to the wider Galatian setting of the letter. There were three types of ancient rhetoric: first, forensic or judicial, that is, of speeches made at civil or criminal trials; secondly, deliberative, that is of essentially political speeches given before public gatherings or legislative assemblies; and, thirdly, epideictic, that is, of occasional or commemorative speeches in praise or blame of someone, for example, funeral orations. In reliance upon the main features of a speech according to the ancient rhetoricians, Betz (1975; 1979) divides Galatians as follows:

(a) 1.1–5 Epistolary prescript.
(b) 1.6–11 *Exordium,* or introduction.
(c) 1.12–2.14 *Narratio,* or statement of facts.
(d) 2.15–21 *Propositio, t*ranslition from *narratio* to *probatio.*
(e) 3.1–4.31 *Probatio,* or statement of proof.
(f) 5.1–6.10 *Exhortatio.*
(g) 6.11–18 Epistolary postscript (*conclusio*).

Betz sees Galatians as primarily analogous to a forensic speech, on the basis that Paul is defending himself and his reputation against attack. The better view (see Hester 1984; Kennedy 1984: 144–52), however, is that it is analogous to a deliberative speech, since Paul is primarily seeking to persuade the Galatians to a particular course of action, or more accurately, to dissuade them from one, namely, submission to the Jewish Law, and what he has to say about himself is subordinated to this aim. Moreover, by its very nature, deliberative rhetoric was divided into exhortation or dissuasion. On the other hand, exhortation was not regarded as a part of judicial rhetoric by the ancient authors. Accordingly, the significance of the *exhortatio* in Galatians (5.1–6.10) looms as a significant obstacle for Betz in trying to view the rhetoric of Galatians as forensic and not deliberative.

Our chief interest lies in the role the *narratio* was thought to play in judicial and deliberative rhetoric. Betz was influenced in his view that Galatians is an example of forensic rhetoric by the prominence of the *narratio* (1.12–2.14). In a forensic speech the *narratio* is usually central as it contains the facts at issue in the dispute. If Betz were correct on this point, it would mean that Paul's autobiographical details, especially concerning his interaction with the Jerusalem leadership in the past, would contain precisely the facts at issue in Galatia. But Betz has gone astray here. In fact, the *narratio* was used in all types of ancient rhetoric (Kennedy 1984: 144–5). Even in deliberative speeches, where they were not as critical as in legal proceedings, *narrationes* were used, although for various purposes (Quintilian, *Institutes* 3.8.10–11 and 4.2.11–12). If Galatians was a forensic speech we would expect to have an account of the facts of Paul's activities in Galatia, not of events in Antioch some years earlier. In a deliberative address, such as Galatians, the point of the *narratio* is to relate matters 'which have a bearing on the case and contribute to an understanding of the speaker, but are not directly in issue' (Kennedy 1984: 145). From this perspective, therefore, we are entitled to regard what happened at Antioch as relevant to the later course of events in Galatia. Thus the canons of ancient rhetoric justify the conclusion that even in a deliberative address there must be some relationship between the *narratio* and the current situation. Nevertheless, it is still necessary to examine the actual details of the text, in the light of its ancient context, to determine the precise nature of the relationship.

In fact, Paul establishes two unequivocal interconnections between the events of the past involving the Jerusalem church and the incident in Antioch, and the experience of his Galatian addressees. First, in relating what led up to the Jerusalem agreement that he could continue to evangelise among the Gentiles, he states that he did not succumb to pressure from conservative opponents, in order 'that the truth of the Gospel might be preserved *for you*' (2.5; my emphasis). In other words, he is directly linking his activities in Jerusalem with the situation of his Galatian readers, by suggesting, rather implausibly, that his actions at some time in the past were actually motivated by his concern for the Galatians. Secondly, during the course of the allegory of Sarah and Hagar (4.21–5.1), Paul argues that Jerusalem and its children, which no doubt includes the church of that city, are in slavery (4.25). This reference to the slavery characterising the Jerusalem church at the time he is writing to the Galatians is matched by his allegation that during the meeting in Jerusalem false Christians of that city had tried 'to spy out our freedom which we have in Christ Jesus, in order that they might enslave us' (2.4; my translation), obviously by seeking to impose circumcision. Accordingly, Paul links the past and the present by asserting that the Jerusalem church, or at least part of it, is a source of slavery. Not quite as clear cut, but nevertheless very revealing, is the consideration that Paul describes the people from fear of whom Peter withdrew from the Gentiles in Antioch as 'those of the circumcision' (*hoi ek peritomēs* – 2.12). The expression also appears in Acts 11.2 of the members of the Jerusalem church who were unhappy that Peter had eaten with Cornelius. Its use in 2.12

is matched by the fact that those who advocate a different Gospel in Galatia are seeking to impose circumcision on the Gentile members there.

This leads us to consider what Paul may have meant by *Ioudaizein*, which is the last word of his report of what he said to Peter before everyone at Antioch and, indeed, the culmination and climax of this whole historical interlude: 'If you, though a Jew, live like a Gentile and not like a Jew, how can you compel the Gentiles to live like Jews (*Ioudaizein*)?' (2.14). Within the Galatian context of the letter, one would assume that this word must here mean to become a Jew or to live like a Jew, but in either case to be circumcised, given the ways, noted above, in which Paul ties the two situations together. H.D. Betz, the author of the leading English commentary on the letter, adopts this meaning and, in fact, reports no other views (1979: 112). When Paul immediately after this passage goes on to say: 'We ourselves, who are Jews by birth and not Gentile sinners, yet who know that a man is not justified by works of the law but through faith in Jesus Christ, even we have believed in Christ Jesus' (2.15–16), it is difficult to avoid the impression that the phrase 'works of the law', which certainly includes circumcision whatever else it means, carries the same connotation as *Ioudaizein*. As we will soon see, however, Professor Dunn interprets *Ioudaizein* quite differently.

We may summarise the point we have now reached as follows:

(a) Paul's opponents in Galatia, Jewish Christians themselves threatened with persecution by non-Christian Jews, were concerned at some aspect of the association between Jews and Gentiles in the local Christian communities.

(b) So seriously did his opponents in Galatia regard the situation that they were encouraging the Gentile members of their communities to be circumcised.

(c) The Jewish Christians may have been threatening to end their association with the Gentiles unless they were to be circumcised and keep the Law.

(d) The earlier problem at Antioch had also involved a breach of association, manifested in particular in the withdrawal by the Jewish Christians from table-fellowship.

(e) That the problem at Antioch in the past was the same as that vexing Paul when he wrote his letter to the Galatians is also possible in view of the status of Gal. 1.12–2.14 as a *narratio*

within the conventions of ancient rhetoric and its close connections with the Galatian situation, whether the letter be
construed as judicial or even as deliberative rhetoric.

(f) If the issue which led Peter and the other Jewish Christians to
break off table-fellowship with the Gentiles in Antioch was the
same as that exercising the Galatian congregations when Paul
wrote the letter, circumcision would probably have been the
only solution from the point of view of the Jewish Christians in
Antioch.

Having now explored the wider context in the Galatian communities for the account Paul gives of the Antioch incident, and
suggested a possible basis for the connection between the two
situations, we may now proceed to the arguments raised by Dunn
and Sanders in connection with the nature of the Antiochean
dispute.

THE DISPUTE AT ANTIOCH

Dunn begins with certain aspects of the relationship between the
church in Jerusalem and the church in Antioch (Dunn 1983 and
1990). He suggests that at the stage of the Antioch incident the
new movement of those who followed Jesus would still have
regarded themselves as a development of and within the religion
of the Jews, not yet a distinct faith or a separate religion. He has in
mind what I call a reform movement within Judaism, to use the
language of the model I outlined in Chapter 1. Dunn's admittedly
prima facie view, it should be noted, fails to address the possibility,
which I raised in relation to the model as it could be applied to the
first followers of Jesus in Jerusalem, that different sectors of the
new movement may have developed in their relationship with
wider Judaism at different stages. I shall be suggesting below that
the very issue at stake in Antioch was that Paul was proposing
something which was inevitably sectarian *vis-à-vis* Judaism, while
the alternative advocated by the Jewish Christians would have left
Christianity as a reform movement within Judaism. Dunn also
suggests that at this time the primacy and authority of the
Jerusalem apostles in matters of dispute would be generally
acknowledged. He then proceeds to the socio-political situation
confronting Judaism in the middle of the first century and
proposes that the increasing threat to Judaism, especially from
the deteriorating political situation, would have increased pres-

sure on those involved in the new movement to show themselves as faithful and loyal Jews.

Dunn next develops, in a characteristically careful and detailed argument, his views on the question of Jewish–Gentile table-fellowship in the Judaism of the Second Temple period. He concludes that there would have been a broad range of social intercourse between faithful Jews and Gentiles, at least those of the God-fearing type, with strict Jews avoiding table-fellowship as far as possible, and those less scrupulous in matters of tithing and purity willingly extending and accepting invitations to meals where such Gentiles were present. Dunn does not consider that there was any problem in principle with Jews dining with God-fearing Gentiles in this period.

I consider that on this matter the evidence Dunn summons does not prove his case and that he fails to account for evidence to the contrary. I do not doubt, nor have I ever doubted, that there was a range of social and commercial intercourse between Jews and Gentiles during the period in question (1987: 84 and 157–8). But the conduct of the eucharist, the *kuriakon deipnon*, raised a quite distinct problem. In my view there was in existence at the time of the Antioch incident a norm of conduct among Jews to the effect that it was wrong to dine with Gentiles if such dining involved the passing around, the handling by all present, of the one loaf of bread and the one cup of wine, which , as I noted earlier, was an essential aspect of eucharistic table-fellowship (1987: 71–86). Contrary to Dunn's view (1990: 180–1), it was quite immaterial whether the Gentile was a God-fearer or not; thus, the fact that Cornelius was a God-fearing Gentile of impeccable credentials (Acts 10.1–2) in no way affected the criticism which a section of the Jerusalem church levelled at Peter because he had eaten with him (Acts 11.3). A person was either a member of the covenant community, as demonstrated by circumcision, or not. There was no *via media* on the question of table-fellowship with Jews.

Because Dunn does not consider that mixed table-fellowship *per se* was the problem, he has to come up with some other issue. His answer is that, prior to the arrival of the people from James, the Gentile believers at Antioch were already observing the basic food laws prescribed by the Jewish Law, such as those prohibiting pork and prescribing proper methods of slaughtering. What the

men from James called for was a much more scrupulous obser-
vance of the dietary laws, especially with regard to ritual purity, by
which he means the extra requirements of the Pharisees (especially as to the cleansing of hands) and tithing. So on this view, all
would have been well in the community at Antioch if the Jews and
Gentiles had washed their hands before eating and if the wheat
from which the eucharistic loaf had been baked and the grapes
for the wine had been properly tithed. My view that this was too
trivial an issue to explain Antioch (1987: 88) has elicited from
Dunn the reply that it was over matters such as these that the
factions within Judaism discounted other Jews as sinners and
apostates (Dunn 1990: 181).

The first enquiry we must make in assessing Dunn's proposal is
how it can be reconciled with the Galatian context of the letter. In
particular, can Dunn be right if the same problem which agitated
the church in Antioch is now agitating the Galatian communities?
Yet Paul's use of the Antioch incident as part of his argument,
unadorned by any other explanation for its presence, would raise
a strong *prima facie* presumption that it was the same issue even in
the absence of the connections, discussed above, which Paul sets
up between the past and the present. As noted earlier, Dunn
surprisingly formulated his view without considered reference to
this matter. A further consideration, moreover, reveals that we
would be virtually compelled to make the unlikely assumption
that the two situations were different if Dunn was correct. Assume
for the moment that it was the same problem. Assume that in the
Galatian communities Jewish and Gentile Christians were engaging in table-fellowship without observing Pharisaical purity
requirements such as hand-washing and without using tithed
bread and wine. Also assume that this could have caused sufficient
consternation in Jewish or Jewish Christian circles to lead to
persecution. What would one expect the solution to be as far as
aggrieved Jewish sentiment was concerned? Simple – 'Wash your
hands before eating, brothers, and pass that tithed bread and
wine.' A slight modification of existing habits and all would be
well. Yet the actual remedy being strongly pursued in Galatia was
circumcision. If the problem was the same in Antioch we would
expect the remedy to be the same as well. In each case there would
be no balance between the problem and its solution. Why pursue
the difficult course of trying to have the Gentiles go through a
painful and, in the days before antibiotics, a potentially

dangerous operation when all that is required is a minor change of behaviour? That would indeed be the use of a sledge-hammer to crack a nut. But even more fatal to the argument is that even if the Gentiles were circumcised the alleged problem of failure to eat like a Pharisee and to tithe would remain!

Dunn's approach necessitates, moreover, that he gives *Ioudaizein* an unlikely meaning. He wants this to mean Judaise in a lesser sense, so that Paul would be merely attributing to Peter a wish to have the Gentiles adopt some less draconian Jewish practices, in particular Pharisaical purity and tithing. As already noted, however, a reader of the letter, at least one who regarded the Antiochean passage as somehow related to the position in Galatia, would tend to assume that this word meant to become a Jew or to live like a Jew in the full sense, including circumcision. Dunn cites some usages of *Ioudaizein* outside of the New Testament which he believes support a meaning for the word which does not involve circumcision, but their testimony is equivocal on the point and in any event it is preferable to be guided by the letter itself in determining the meaning.

These reflections strongly suggest that if Dunn is correct the problem in Galatia was quite different in nature from that in Antioch. This would mean that Paul's insertion of the Antiochean material, without anything to suggest how it might possibly be relevant to the Galatians, was an entirely pointless and otiose act on his part. Clearly, the preferable course is to seek an interpretation which makes sense of this unexplained insertion. The least problematic view is that the same problem was present in both situations. This means Dunn's proposal must be rejected as irreconcilable with the Galatian context.

A second objection to Dunn's explanation is that it is difficult to square with what Paul describes as having occurred in Antioch itself. If ritual purity and tithing were the issues they would have affected both Jews and Gentiles in the community. To solve the alleged problem of such requirements not being met both groups would have had to agree to their implementation. This would presumably have involved a meeting to assess the attitudes of everyone on the issue. If no agreement could be reached then perhaps there might have been a Jewish walkout, although even then some of the Gentiles might have agreed to the new requirements anyway. But Paul describes nothing like this. First there was mixed table-fellowship, next the arrival of the men from James and then all of the Jews withdrew, led by fear, out of fear of the circumcision party. One gains the distinct impression that nothing along the lines of a discussion took place and this suggests that it was the very fact of the practice and not the manner in which it was conducted that caused the problem.

A third objection to Dunn's view comes from the response of E.P. Sanders, whose arguments on the point may be summarised as two propositions: first, no-one anywhere ever thought that Antiochene Jews should not eat until they had sent some of their food to the Temple, although such Jews did at times send voluntary offerings; and, secondly, there is no evidence to suppose that in Antioch Jews were under pressure from Pharisees to raise purity standards (Sanders 1990: 172). The Jewish evidence suggests that Pharisees did not try to impose their special rules on others. Sanders's argument, based on the Jewish material external to the text, that Dunn's proposal does not explain the problem, corroborates the same view we have reached through a consideration of the terms of the letter itself.

THE PROHIBITION ON TABLE-FELLOWSHIP

Sanders's own explanation for what underlay the controversy at Antioch was that 'strict' Jews might be reluctant to to associate too much with Gentiles, since close association might lead to contact with idolatry or transgression of one of the biblical food laws. He sees this as not involving a law, but a worry about the results of fraternisation. He also suggests that there may have been a general dislike on James' part of eating Gentile food and that Peter's mission would be discredited if he were known to engage in it himself. On this view, as on mine, the problem in Antioch lay with the very practice of mixed table-fellowship. Although Sanders disagrees with my conclusion that there was a prohibition on the practice in first-century Judaism, his conclusion that there was a disinclination to eat with Gentiles, even if there was thought to be no law against it, is much closer to my view on the matter than it is to Dunn's.

In spite of Sanders' views, I would wish to insist, as I have long maintained, that as far as Jewish–Gentile table-fellowship was concerned, 'in the full sense of sitting around a table with them and sharing the same food, wine and vessels' (Esler 1987: 84), actually handling the one loaf and drinking from the same cup, there was a strong body of Jewish opinion at this time that this was prohibited under the law. This does not mean that there were not occasions when Jews did breach this prohibition, just as they breached the specific requirements of the law promulgated by Moses, but it does mean there was a norm on the subject whose breach was likely to cause serious affront and pressure to terminate the practice and that there was, in fact, widespread compliance with it.

It is not possible within the confines of this work to go into this question in detail, let alone to reply to Sanders's unsatisfactory criticism of my position, so I shall deal only with a few aspects of the matter. The primary source of the prohibition was the need to maintain those parts of the Torah enjoining idolatry, especially Exod. 23.13, 23.24, 23.32–3 and 34.12–16, and Deut. 7.1–5, 7.25–6 and 12.2–3. Gentiles, of course, were likely to be deeply implicated in idolatry, so great care had to be taken in dealing with them. On the other hand, some intercourse with Gentiles was always likely to be necessary for commercial reasons and when they atttended synagogue, as so many of them did. Reconciling the tension between these two issues exercised the Jewish tradition for centuries. The Mishnah (especially the tractate '*Abodah Zarah*) and the Gemara frequently indicate the necessity of differentiating between Gentiles as idolaters and Gentiles as business or social associates (see Porton 1988: 241–58). But these sources exhibit a virtual obsession on the question of Gentile wine, which was regarded as routinely dedicated to pagan gods by making a small libation. The question arises then of how a Jew could sit with a Gentile and take from him or her the eucharistic cup without possibly being a party to idolatry. Even Sanders concedes, although apparently without appreciating its significance for mixed Jewish–Gentile table-fellowship, that there 'was no barrier to social intercourse with Gentiles, as long as one did not eat their meat or drink their wine' (Sanders 1990: 178). This prohibition had the social function of protecting Jewish ethnic identity in a Gentile world.

In spite of Dunn's recent endorsement of a statement by A.F. Segal that 'there is no law in rabbinic literature that prevents a Jew from eating with a gentile' (Dunn 1991: 306, n. 61), there is *halakah* on point in the Tosefta '*Abodah Zarah* 4.6, in the saying of Rabbi Shimeon ben Eleazar (of the late second century CE) to the effect that Jews who dined in a Gentile's house committed idolatry, even though they ate their own food and wine and their own servants served it to them! This type of prohibition underlies what Peter says, in the context of entering the house of Cornelius and inevitably engaging in table-fellowship with him: 'You know that it is *athemitos* ['prohibited on religious grounds'] for a Jew to visit or associate with a non-Jew' (Acts 10.28). As already noted, the fact that Cornelius was a God-fearer made no difference to the hostility which Peter's eating with him stirred up in the Jerusalem church, as Luke records in Acts 11.3.

CONCLUSION

We are now in a position to explain the nature of the controversy in Antioch. Paul advocated eucharistic table-fellowship between Jews and Gentiles. His reason for doing so was almost certainly a theological one: through faith the membership had come to share in the redemption won by Christ as demonstrated by the activity of the Holy Spirit (Gal. 3.2–5). This occurred without distinction as between Jew and Gentile. For anyone to come along after this had happened and claim that circumcision and the law were necessary involved the corollary that Christ was not sufficient. As Paul says in Gal. 2.21: 'If justification were through the law, then Christ died to no purpose.' In Christ all were one, whether Jew or Gentile, slave or free, male or female (Gal. 3.28). This was a theological truth, yet the social expression and confirmation of the opening of salvation to all regardless of such categories was eucharistic table-fellowship. To oppose this practice, as far as Paul was concerned, meant annulling the achievement of Christ. And this he could not allow. He insisted on mixed table-fellowship at all costs, even if this resulted in a decisive rift with the Jews, or, in modern parlance, a sectarian position with respect to the mother faith. From the Jewish Christian point of view, on the other hand, the practice of Jews and Gentiles sitting at table and passing around the one loaf and the one cup involved a dereliction from the commandment against idolatry, or, just as bad, seemed to Jewish outsiders to involve such a dereliction. The fact that mixed table-fellowship was thought to be idolatrous explains the pitch of animosity against it. Their understandable solution was to have the Gentiles circumcised and then the problem would cease to exist. Christianity would then remain a messianic reform movement within Judaism.

Paul's subsequent problem in Galatia was that other people had come along after him, almost certainly connected with Jerusalem (Gal. 4.25), running the same argument as before that there must be no table-fellowship between Jew and Gentile. For the Gentiles not to be excluded (*ekkleisai* - 4.17) they had to be circumcised and carry out the requirements of the law. In other words, they were required to become Jews. Paul saw the attempt to impose the law on his Gentile converts as a different Gospel. With a pervasive sense of *déjà vu*, he referred the Galatians back to the source and legitimacy of his apostleship, its recognition by the Jerusalem authorities, the agreement in Jerusalem and the incident in Antioch. There the issue had been the same, an initial engaging in mixed fellowship, followed by a conservative Jewish reaction to it to reassert the established prohibition unless the Gentiles became circumcised. In Galatia as in Antioch, Paul advocated a type of Christianity inevitably sectarian in relation to Judaism.

One final point. The word 'persecute' (*diōkein*) is employed with respect to the persecution in Galatia impending on those who do not have the Gentiles circumcised (6.12), of Paul's addressees (4.29), of some persecution directed at Paul himself (5.11) and of Paul's own persecution of the early church (1.13, 23). In the first three cases the persecution is related to the issue of circumcision. The first two must, on the views advanced here, also be related to table-fellowship and the third one may be. From this we ask, given the uniformity of the background to all other usages of *diōkein* in this letter, may we not also see Paul's persecution of the early church in the same light? Is the long-standing puzzle of why the early community should have been persecuted at all and by Paul in particular to be solved on the basis that it was aimed at stamping out the very same practice of Jewish–Gentile eucharistic fellowship which later vexed the communities of Antioch and Galatia? This presupposes the admission of Gentiles into the congregations at a very early date, but I have set out a possible basis for such a phenomenon elsewhere (1987: 155–63).

Chapter 5

Introverted sectarianism at Qumran and in the Johannine community

THE DUALISM OF THE COMMUNITY RULE FROM QUMRAN AND THE FOURTH GOSPEL

The Community Rule, one of the most significant of the Dead Sea scrolls, and the Gospel of John exhibit an outlook which is noticeably dualistic. The Community Rule (referred to as '1QS'), for example, describes at one point how God, having created human beings to rule the world, assigned two spirits to them until the appointed time of his visitation, a spirit of truth and a spirit of injustice. The passage continues:

> From a spring of light come the generations of truth, and from a well of darkness the generations of injustice. Control over all the sons of righteousness lies in the hand of the prince of lights, and they walk in the ways of light; complete control over the sons of injustice lies in the hand of the angel of darkness, and they walk in the ways of darkness. It is through the angel of darkness that all the sons of righteousness go astray. All their afflictions and their times of distress are brought about by his rule of hatred, and all the spirits of his lot make the sons of light to stumble.
>
> (1QS III.19–24; Knibb 1987: 95)

After this the text recounts the particular types of behaviour which characterise those who are led by either spirit (1QS IV.2–11) and the fate destined for each group (1QS IV.15–26). Similarly, in John's Gospel we find a pronounced dualism between the world above and the world below, between the force of the world above (represented by Christ) and the force of the one below (represented especially by the Jews), and between light and dark-

darkness, which characterise the two worlds (see Charlesworth 1990: 89–91 for details).

The dualism found in the Community Rule and the Johannine Gospel is not easily paralleled in other Jewish or Christian documents from the first century CE. This rarity leads us to seek some explanation for its presence in each and, moreover, to assess whether there may have been some kind of connection between the two works. Many commentators have previously sought to address these issues using established techniques of historical investigation. In the research on this matter published to date, moreover, there has been a tendency to treat the perspective in the Community Rule as a given and then to propose how John or his tradition could have come into contact with the Qumran material and been influenced by it (Charlesworth 1990; Ashton 1991). The methodology adopted in this book, however, necessitates the amplification of historical method with social-scientific ideas and approaches. Accordingly, in this chapter I will investigate the Community Rule and the Fourth Gospel from a social-scientific perspective. Although this will initially necessitate the application of the sociology of sectarianism in a general way to the communities for whom the documents were written, my ultimate aim is to determine whether such a method offers any new solution to the dualism evident in these two texts.

THE SECTARIAN TYPOLOGY OF BRYAN WILSON

The sectarianism which has occupied our attention in previous chapters has been of the type which has resulted from breach with a parent church. A sect may achieve its identity, however, more in relation to the world at large than to any particular religion. Such is the case with many sects which have sprung up recently in Western countries. A useful method of classifying a wide range of sectarian phenomena, capable of dealing with cases where a church has or has not been the context in which the sect arose, has been developed by Bryan R. Wilson, an English sociologist. This classification takes the form of a seven-part typology and has gone through several editions. The edition which I will use, which appears in his *Magic and the Millennium* (1975), has been heavily influenced by Third World religious movements. My aim is to explore the usefulness of this typology in explaining certain aspects of the responses to the world manifested by the Qumran and Johannine communities, including the dualism evident in both.

A sectarian movement, according to Wilson, always manifests some degree of tension with the world, where 'world' may include the dominant religious tradition (as in the cases considered in this chapter) or, as with many contemporary sects, society at large. Accordingly, each sect exhibits some form of 'response to the world' which expresses both what its members find inadequate in the existing order and the strategies and ideology they propound in its stead. Wilson's typology consists of seven broad responses to the world: conversionist, revolutionist, introversionist, manipulationist, thaumaturgical, reformist and utopian. Each such type is an ideal-construct, used for the purposes of comparison, and not necessarily a description of any particular empirical phenomenon. Moreover, any given religious movement may be comparable with more than one of the seven types, although generally one of them will offer richer materials for comparative purposes than the others.

In the present context, the two most useful of Wilson's types are the 'revolutionist' and the 'introversionist'. He describes the revolutionist response as follows:

> A second response to evil is to declare that only the destruction of the world, of the natural, but more specifically of the social, order, will suffice to save men. This process of destruction must be supernaturally wrought, for men lack the power if not to destroy the world then certainly to re-create it . . . the outworking of the prophesied cataclysm and subsequent restoration is essentially the doing of supernatural agencies . . . In this case men may not claim to be saved now but do claim that they will *very soon* be saved: salvation is imminent. No subjective reorientation will affect the state of the world: its objective condition must be recognised. It will only be changed by divine action.
>
> (Wilson 1975: 23)

The phenomena Wilson labels 'revolutionist' are similar to those referred to by other writers as 'millennial'. He describes the introversionist response as follows:

> The third response . . . is to see the world as irredeemably evil and salvation to be attained only by the fullest possible withdrawal from it. The self may be purified by renouncing the

world and leaving it. This response might be an individual response, of course, but as the response of a social movement it leads to the establishment of a separated community preoccupied with its own holiness and its means of insulation from the wider society. Even if the ideology posits only its future realisation, in practice, salvation is sociologically a *present* endeavour. The community itself becomes the source and seat of all salvation. Explicitly this prospect of salvation is only for those who belong.

(Wilson 1975: 23-4)

The separation at the heart of this response may be geographical or social.

Sometimes sectarian movements pass from a revolutionist phase to an introversionist phase as a way of coming to terms with the failure of millennial expectation. On the other hand, Wilson notes that among certain less-developed peoples introversionist movements, often led by a quietist prophet, sometimes appear without such a background (Wilson 1975: 384-5 and 387). His or her message is largely ethical, and is often ethnically circumscribed. Here a prophet promises little more than the maintenance of a separate way of life now, and ultimate good in some future dispensation, which might be heavenly or terrestrial. An example of this type of introversionism, to be discussed in more detail in Chapter 7, is the religion developed at the very end of the eighteenth century by an Iroquois Indian, Handsome Lake, which assisted his tribe to cope with life as a dominated minority. There was an eschatological aspect to the foundational visions of Handsome Lake, but the End was not expected for three generations, which seems to have been interpreted as 300 years. In the meantime, what mattered was the quiet fulfilment of ethical obligations. The threat of eschatological horrors was really used to reinforce the ethics of the religion (Wilson 1975: 387-97).

THE ESSENES AT QUMRAN AND IN ISRAEL

Discussion of the ancient scrolls found in the late 1940s and early 1950s in eleven caves near Khirbet Qumran on the shores of the Dead Sea is agitated by controversy over two critical issues: first, whether there was a connection between the inhabitants of Qumran and the scrolls, or more particularly, whether the scrolls constituted the library of a community of pious Jews who lived there; and, secondly, if there was such a connection, whether the inhabitants of Qumran are to be identified with the Essenes known to us from certain ancient authors (usefully collected in Vermes and Goodman 1989). The first issue is intrinsically linked with the archaeological excavation of the site conducted by a team led by Roland de Vaux from the Dominican École Biblique in Jerusalem in the 1950s. Unfortunately, it appears to be the case that the excavators, perhaps because of their own background, were too quick to interpret what they found as a type of Jewish monastery. Thus, the famous feature which they reconstructed as the long writing desk of a monastic scriptorium has recently been reassessed by the archaeologists now preparing the final report on the site as a triclinium, a dining couch (Donceel-Voûte 1992). Moreover, the excavators do not seem to have paid sufficient attention to evidence of certain commercial activities on the site, for example, glass-making. Some of these difficulties might have become apparent if the excavators, rather than publishing their findings in de Vaux's Schweich lectures on the site (de Vaux 1973) and other shorter notices, had themselves prepared a final report, which regrettably they did not. Only in recent years has that task begun in earnest, but in the meantime some of the materials excavated, many of the coins, for example, have disappeared (Donceel-Voûte 1992). In spite of these reservations, many scholars continue to believe that the most plausible explanation for the discovery of so many scrolls so close to Qumran was that they were owned by a community living there, even if it is necessary to situate its membership more concretely in the commercial activities of the region. The fact that the scrolls are written in a large number of different hands is explicable on the basis that some of them at least were brought to Qumran by persons who joined the community and allowed them to become communal property. Norman Golb's hypothesis, that the scrolls were brought from the Temple in Jerusalem around 70 CE to keep them safe at the time of the war with the Romans (Golb 1980 and 1985), labours under the twin difficulties of explaining the coincidence that the hiding place chosen, of all the possible refuges in Palestine, just happened to be Qumran and of accounting for the fact that those responsible for the scrolls would have thought Qumran a safer place than behind the walls of Jerusalem. Moreover, one of the Qumran scrolls, the Community Rule, actually envisages a religious movement retiring to the desert:

When these exist as a community in Israel in accordance with these rules, they shall separate themselves from the settlement of the men of injustice and shall go into the wilderness to prepare there for the way of him, as it is written: 'In the wilderness prepare the way of . . . make level in the desert a highway for our God.' This way is the study of the law which he commanded through Moses.

(1QS VIII.12–15; Knibb 1987: 128)

If 1QS had been discovered somewhere else, in an old monastery, for example, the most plausible explanation for its origin would have been in a religious community which had retired to the Palestinian desert for the intensive study of the Mosaic law. In other words, even if we knew nothing of Qumran we would have been forced to invent something very like it!

As to the second question raised initially, the relationship between the owners of the scrolls and the Essenes, it seems to me that the better view is that they are essentially identical. Apart from pronounced similarities in their lifestyles as described by Josephus, Pliny the Elder and Philo (who calls them Essaeans) compared with what we can observe in some of the scrolls, Pliny the Elder actually locates the Essenes on the west shore of the Dead Sea, between Jericho and Engedi, which points to Qumran (*Natural History* 5.17.4; Vermes 1989: 32-3). Nevertheless, it is important that in dealing with the Essenes we distinguish between those who lived in communities throughout Israel and those who resided at Qumran (or whatever desert community we must postulate as the source of 1QS). For the former group we have the description in the literary texts and the information contained in the Damascus Document. For the inhabitants of Qumran we have most significantly for present purposes 1QS, the Rule of the Congregation ('1QSA') and the War Rule ('1QM' and '4QM') together with some of the material in the literary descriptions. The initial question is to determine whether the religious manifestations they reflect are sectarian. If so, we may proceed to apply Wilson's typology in the way previously explained. I will begin with the groups referred to in the Damascus Document.

THE DAMASCUS DOCUMENT

Although fragments of this work turned up in Caves 4, 5 and 6 at Qumran (Knibb 1987: 13), which demonstrated its interest for those who lived there, it had been known much earlier, since it was found among the medieval manuscripts which were discovered in a storeroom of the Cairo synagogue at the end of the nineteenth century. The parts of it which survived were published by S. Schechter in 1910 under the title *Fragments of a Zadokite Work*. Some aspects of the Damascus Document ('CD' – referring to the Cairo manuscripts of the Damascus Document) show signs of a relationship with certain other documents found at Qumran, especially the Community Rule. It may be that an earlier form of CD has been redacted to bring it into greater harmony with the outlook at Qumran (Davies 1982: 176ff).

By and large CD bears witness to a religious movement with some prominent divergences from the religious orientation evident in certain Qumran documents, namely, 1QS, the Rule of the Congregation and the War Rule. Most notably, it provides for the existence of communities ('camps') following its ordinances which are presumably located throughout Israel. In this regard it matches the description which Josephus provides of the Essenes as living in each city (*Jewish War* II.124) and the report of Philo that they lived in many cities and villages in Judaea (quoted in Eusebius, *Praeparatio Evangelica* VIII.II.I). 1QS, on the other hand, speaks of retirement to the wilderness and this indicates a rather different orientation. In the light of the model outlined in Chapter 1, the initial question arising from this aspect of CD is whether it is properly described as a sect or a reform movement in relation to Judaism. I cannot share the confidence expressed by Professor Graham Stanton recently that 'There can be no doubt at all that the Damascus Document comes from a sectarian community' (Stanton 1992: 91). As we shall see, 1QS, however, does represent a sectarian form of Judaism.

A number of images are employed in CD to indicate that the movement for which it was written has a social identity separate from that of wider Israel. Its members are designated as 'all who enter the covenant' (II.2) and it is clear that the ordinances of their covenant include but go beyond the Mosaic Law. They are described as a remnant (II.11) and in one passage it is said that 'God built for them a sure house in Israel' (III.19). Their local communities, or cells, are called 'camps' (*makhanot* - VIII.6, XIX.20), which vividly connotes their sense of differentiation from Israel since this was the expression used of the settlements of the Israelites when they were in the wilderness (Exod. 16.13; Num. 2.17).

In addition to their distinctive ideology and social identity, there are unambiguous signs of antipathy between the covenanters and the Judaism contemporary with them of the type which often accompanies the interaction between a reform movement and its parent church. Thus CD attacks Israel for being ensnared in three 'nets of Belial', namely, certain forms of sexual malpractice, an obsession with wealth and defiling the Temple. The opponents of the movement are said to have 'defiled their holy spirits' (V.11). In one passage the leaders of Israel, referred to as 'the princes of Judah' (VIII.3), are subjected to a sustained attack (VIII.2–13) in terms which suggest, as Davies notes, 'that the religious/political authorities outside the community are exercising a competing claim for the loyalty of newly-arrived members' (1982: 119). At the same time, the members of the covenant have themselves been criticised by persons apparently representative of wider Israel: 'with a blasphemous tongue [they] have opened their mouths against the ordinances of God's covenant, saying that it is not established' (V.11-12). The possibility that external pressure of this kind might have an influence on the membership is suggested in the dire warnings offered to those who become apostates:

> all the men who entered the new covenant in the land of Damascus and have turned back and acted treacherously and departed from the well of living water shall not be reckoned in the 'council of the people' and shall not be written in their records from the time of the Teacher.
>
> (XIX.33b–35)

Although Davies considers this to be one of the interpolated passages (1982: 176), it reveals the precise risk against which the leadership of a breakaway religious group must legitimate, that is, explain and justify, its lifestyle and beliefs to the membership.

In spite of features such as these, which are capable of being construed as indicating a sectarian status for the covenanters, other features of the text render the question more difficult. First and foremost is the fact that although the movement was in dispute with the Temple authorities, parts of CD imply a continued use of the Temple by the community, in the form of offering sacrifice there (see VI.11–16; so Davies 1982: 130). At

XIV.17–18 it is stated: 'Let no man offer on the altar on the Sabbath except the burnt-offering of the Sabbath.' The fact that others might have defiled the Temple does not seem to have been regarded as a reason for the covenanters not sacrificing there. Moreover, as Davies notes, the respects in which CD states that the Temple has been defiled do not appear to be terribly serious ones. They consist of engaging in intercourse with menstruating women and marrying within restricted grades of relationship (Davies 1982: 115). On the other hand, one passage in CD (VI.11–16) does have the effect of preventing any of the covenanters themselves taking part as priests or levites in the Temple cult. The passage begins as follows: 'None of those brought into the covenant shall enter the sanctuary to kindle fire upon his altar in vain' (VI.11; Knibb 1987: 51)

The evidence in CD for involvement by the covenanters in the Temple cult is reinforced by recent archaeological excavations suggesting that there was an Essene quarter on the south-west hill of Jerusalem. Josephus situates an 'Essene Gate' in this area, which we now know from archaeological study was let into the wall early in the reign of Herod the Great (see Bahat 1970; Capper 1983; Pixner 1983). The fact that there may have been members of the movement behind CD living in Jerusalem is also supported by the following statement in its legal section: 'Let no man lie with a woman in the city of the sanctuary so as to convey uncleanness to the [city of the] sanctuary with their impurity' (XII.1–2; Rabin 1954: 58).

Another feature of CD raising a question over its sectarian status is the fact that it contains regulations as to how one might deal with Gentiles. Two of these may be cited: 'Let no man sell clean beasts and birds to gentiles, in order that they may not sacrifice them. But from his threshing-floor and from his winepress let him not sell anything to them in any circumstances' (XII.9–10; Rabin 1954: 60). In the light of my discussion in Chapter 4 on table-fellowship, it is interesting to see here a total prohibition on the sale of grain and wine to Gentiles. Elsewhere it is said, 'Let no man of all the members of the covenant of God trade with the children of the Pit except for cash' (XIII.14–15; Rabin 1954: 66). It is clear from this, first, that individual members owned their own farms and other businesses and, secondly, that there must have been scope for commerce with the Gentiles (Rabin's comment to the contrary at 1954: 67 is inexplicable).

These features convey an impression of the covenanters having a very different response to the outside world than that evident at Qumran and one not so readily termed sectarian.

One final point should be made here. Although both 1QS and the War Rule contain strongly dualistic language and concepts, this language is not nearly so prominent in CD. In particular, the basic division in the world between the sons of light and the sons of darkness referred to in 1QS and the War Rule is not found in CD at all.

From this investigation I am hesitant to describe the people for whom CD was written as sectarian. They are more appropriately described as a reform movement. They have some elements of isolationism in their outlook, but the fact that they continue to attend the Temple and to interact with Gentiles makes it difficult to call them sectarian.

INTROVERTED SECTARIANISM AT QUMRAN

The initial question raised by the social-scientific perspectives under discussion is whether the Qumran branch of the movement was sectarian *vis-à-vis* Judaism. In one part of the Community Rule, mentioned above, which seems to contain very old material because it sets the establishment of the settlement in the wilderness in the future (1QS VIII.1–16), reference is made to the creation of a council of the community of twelve men and three priests all perfect in the ways of the law, 'that they may pay for iniquity by the practice of justice and [the endurance of] the distress of affliction'. The council will be 'a most holy dwelling for Aaron, with eternal knowledge of the covenant of justice, and shall offer a soothing odour; and [it shall be] a house of perfection and truth in Israel'. In other words, it will function as a kind of alternative Temple. Here we have a classic example of a religious reform movement protesting at, and responding to, what is perceived to be injustice and sinfulness by developing new social structures and an ideology which included revitalisation of existing halakhic tradition combined with certain new elements. But the passage also envisages a time when the split between the rest of Judaism and the new movement becomes irrevocable, when 'they shall separate themselves from the men of injustice and shall go into the wilderness to prepare there the way of him' by studying the Mosaic Law. At this point of separation – which, as we shall see, was to be reinforced by barriers thrown up in the way of anyone wishing to join – the new movement comes close to being sectarian. Other aspects confirm the sectarian nature of the group. As already noted, 1QS manifests a powerfully dualistic outlook, especially in the teaching on the two spirits (III.17–IV.1), where we find a clear enunciation of the notion of the basic division between the sons of light and the sons of darkness not found in CD.

The comparability of Wilson's introversionist response to this group is readily apparent. The world is seen as irredeemably evil and salvation depends upon withdrawal from it. The dissatisfaction of the movement at Qumran with the Temple cult probably exceeds that found in CD, since here we find the community establishing itself as a substitute for the Temple. The Qumran writings have an attitude to the outside world far more negative than that in CD. Several types of derogatory expression are used of outsiders. As common as condemnations of the outside world are invocations to separate oneself from it. The rituals by which such separation was achieved and maintained constitute the primary justification for seeing this as an introversionist sect. In particular, the rules of the Qumran community prescribed an extraordinarily elaborate succession of procedures for gaining admission to the community and staying in it thereafter.

To understand these procedures assistance is gained from Arnold Van Gennep's *The Rites of Passage* (1960). Van Gennep distinguished three phases, or forms of rite, in ritual complexes which brought individuals from one place, or life-stage, or group to another. First, there were rites of separation from the previous world, the pre-liminal stage. Next came rites of transition, the liminal stage, when the individual stood on ambiguous ground between the old world and the new, but in preparation for the new. Thirdly, there were the rites of incorporation, the post-liminal stage, which signalled the aggregation of the individual into the new social world. Each of these phases can be seen with great clarity in the process, described in the Community Rule, whereby a person was initiated into full membership of the Qumran community. Upon arrival at Qumran a candidate was examined by the officer in charge with respect to his insights and deeds (1QS VI.14). No doubt failure at this point would have meant departure from Qumran. If the candidate was suitable, the officer admitted him 'into the covenant' (1QS VI.15), which seems to have involved the swearing of an oath to return to the Law of Moses as understood in the community and to separate himself from the outside world, 'the men of injustice who walk in the way of wickedness' (1QS V.7–11). The examination and oath constitute the rite of separation. Thereafter the candidate entered upon an involved series of procedures which functioned as a rite of transition. First of all, he underwent a period of instruction for an unspecified time culminating in an examination (1QS VI.15–16). Secondly, if accepted, the candidate was required to take a year of training, during which he was not allowed to touch the community's 'purity', probably meaning its ritually pure food, nor share in its wealth (1QS VI.15–16). Thirdly, if he passed this test, he handed his property to the overseer (although it was kept separate from the assets of the community) and began a second year of training, during which time he could apparently eat the food of the community, but not drink its drink. Such a ban on drink seems to reflect a belief that liquids were more susceptible to impurity than solids (Knibb 1987: 122). This second year also ended with an examination. If he was successful he could be registered as a full member of the community (1QS VI.21–3). So ended the liminal stage of his separation. The third stage of incorporation involved both the pooling of his property (1QS I.16–II.25) and his formal entry into the community in what appears to have been an annual ceremony for new members to join and for existing members to renew their membership. This ceremony consisted of a protracted series of blessings and curses by priests and Levites. The community members were blessed and any backsliders were cursed. Such a procedure dramatically emphasised the distinction between those inside the community and those outside.

It is difficult to imagine a community which was more preoccupied with its own 'apartness', its 'holiness', or which could go to greater lengths than this one to distinguish itself from everyone else. In short, it is hard to envisage any response to the world more introversionist than this. Yet to understand the stages of the initiation process which so contributed to such introversionism it is necessary to consider the structure of the Temple. The Temple was arranged in a series of courts one within the other which constituted, in effect, concentric zones of holiness. As one moved from the outer court to the Holy of Holies, the class of persons who could enter became narrower and narrower. The successive stages through which a candidate for admission to the Qumran community passed, which clearly reflect a movement from the impurity of the outside world to the purity of the congregation, parallel the journey which one took in passing from the outer court of the Temple to the Holy of Holies. I suspect this parallel was deliberate. The community saw itself as a new Temple and it was almost inevitable that the method of gaining membership to it would be modelled on the means of obtaining access to the Holy of Holies. If the parallel was not deliberate, we would have a case of a typically Jewish attitude to religious experience manifesting itself in a very similar way in two different institutions.

It should be noted, moreover, that the sharp demarcation between the parts of the Temple and the equally sharp demarcation between the persons who could enter those parts reflected a passionate Jewish interest in boundaries and in their preservation which has attracted considerable attention from anthropologists, such as Mary Douglas (1966). The concern with boundaries also surfaces in the Levitical food laws and in the prohibition against eating with, and marrying, Gentiles. What we find with the people at Qumran (and also with the Pharisees and their *haburot* = religious communities) is that the intensification of religious beliefs and practices *vis-à-vis* non-members almost inevitably involved erecting between themselves and other Jews the kind of boundaries which Jews had previously erected between themselves and Gentiles. A sectarian microcosm parallels the larger Jewish macrocosm.

The last issue to be addressed in the comparison is the question of eschatology. Introversionist sectarians tend to regard salvation as a present reality. Even if their ideology posits some future divine transformation of the world, that is not normally seen as imminent and may, indeed, function to reinforce ethical teaching. The community itself becomes the source and seat of salvation. On the other hand, the revolutionist response to the world involves a passionate belief that salvation will come in the future and that the longed-for transformation may well be imminent.

Among Qumran scholars it is something of a commonplace that the movement looked forward to an imminent End. Lawrence Schiffman, in his recent work *The Eschatological Community of the Dead Sea Scrolls*, for example, assumes that this is the case (1989: 7). We must test this view with respect to the branches of the movement represented in CD and in the other Qumran documents. There are several references in CD to God's coming visitation to punish the wicked and reward the good (VII.9, VIII.2–3 and XIX.10, 15), but 'the time of visitation' (XIX.10) is not expressed to be imminent. The references to God's visitation remind the readers of the document that their enemies are in for a nasty time indeed, that God is on their side. This is a transparent form of legitimation that one sees regularly in religious conflict. Its function is to undergird the existence of the community in the present, not really to say anything about the future. On one occasion, however, a prediction of the fate in store for the wicked is accompanied by the blessings which will attend those who hold fast to the rules of the community and obey the Teacher (XIX.15–34). Here we see the characteristic role of eschatology in introversionist movements to reinforce ethics. The interest is in the present, not the future.

It is clear that the members of the movement at Qumran did exhibit certain beliefs which appear more akin to the revolutionist than the introversionist response. They shared with other Jewish groups a belief in the coming judgement and even thought that they were living in 'the last days'. This expression occurs in the Florilegium, another Qumran document. A variety of messianic figures were expected, especially the messiahs of Aaron and Israel and the prophet. In 1QSA they made provision for the rule of the community at 'the end of days'. For all of this, references to an imminent End are not easy to find.

There are certain correspondences, carefully explicated by Schiffman, between arrangements at the end-time and those which are to obtain in the community in the meantime. He sees these correspondences as reflecting an imminent End. I would like to suggest that just the opposite is the case. The more a community does to set up its present arrangements as a reflection of what is expected at the *eschaton*, the less relevant the *eschaton* has become. Similarly, I do not find that the elaborate descriptions in the War Rule of the coming battle between the forces of good, especially the community, and the forces of evil convey any real sense that such a conflict was imminent. Rather, the detailed account of the campaign functions to make its significance symbolically present to the community in its current existence. Just as Mircea Eliade has argued in *The Myth of the Eternal Return* (first published in 1954) that much myth has the effect of recreating the glories of the primordial past in the present, so too can a futurist myth such as we have in the War Rule allow the community direct and contemporary access to its meaning.

Although a belief in the destruction of the present unjust order and the dawn of the messianic age was certainly a part of Qumran ideology, I wish to suggest that this was not its central focus. That this was the case is a reflection of an introversionist outlook. Salvation has become a present endeavour, rather than a future hope. The community believed they were already a holy and almost perfect community, a community of God, closely linked with heaven; as 1QS says: 'He has joined their assembly to the Sons of Heaven to be a Council of the Community, a foundation of the Building of Holiness, an eternal Plantation throughout all ages to come' (1QS XI.7b–9a; Vermes 1975: 93). Pressures which might lead a deprived and oppressed group to generate a millennial dream and long for its fulfilment became considerably attenuated for this community given that it had effectively insulated itself from the evils of the outside world and enjoyed sufficient material possessions and a clear delineation of roles and statuses among its members. For these reasons therefore, although the ideology of the sect at Qumran had a revolutionist flavour, it appears more akin to the introversionist response in regarding salvation as a matter for the present rather than the future.

INTRODUCED SECTARIANISM IN THE JOHANNINE COMMUNITY

Enquiry as to whether the community for whom John wrote his Gospel was sectarian *vis-à-vis* Judaism inevitably begins with J. Louis Martyn's watershed 1968 publication *History and Theology in the Fourth Gospel*. Although on its face this Gospel is an account of what Jesus said and did, Martyn showed how John's account was shaped by the circumstances of his audience, especially a profound Jewish–Christian conflict which had resulted in the expulsion of Christians who were contemporary with John from the synagogue. It is noteworthy that the word *aposynagogos*, which literally means '[expelled] from the synagogue', actually appears on three occasions in the Fourth Gospel (9.22, 12.42 and 16.2). This data in the text substantiates the view that John's community had, indeed, assumed a sectarian status in relation to the Judaism of their time. Influenced by Martyn, but pursuing his own highly original line of research was Wayne A. Meeks. In an article published in 1972, which I mentioned in Chapter 1, Meeks related the critical theological theme in John's Gospel of the descending and ascending redeemer to the sectarian nature of the Johannine community. Oddly enough, in spite of the brilliance of Meeks' analysis, few scholars have developed his insights. A recent exception is David Rensberger, in *Overcoming the World: Politics and Community in the Gospel of John* (1989).

The initial question is the extent to which the community for whom the Gospel was written sees the world as irredeemably evil and salvation to be obtained by withdrawing from it. In this context the 'world' largely means, as we will see, Judaism. It is reasonably certain that the Johannine community was located in one of the cities of the Graeco-Roman East so that the geographic withdrawal which was so significant at Qumran has no place here. Nevertheless, this community provides an excellent example of the way in which a sect may distance itself from the outside world by myth, symbolism and ideology, as much as by geographic space. To illustrate this process I will consider two elements in the symbolical boundaries erected by the community: Jewish attacks on the life of Jesus and the controversy over Abraham in 8.31–59, which has recently been the focus of my own research on John.

Apart from the action by the Jewish authorities which led to his crucifixion at Roman hands, Jewish attacks on Jesus are very rare in the Synoptic Gospels. The only example, in fact, is found at Luke 4.29. The extent to which an evangelist presents Jews as having been hostile to Jesus plainly has the potential to be a useful gauge of the animosity between his own community and Judaism, because of the tendency in the tradition to read disputes contemporary with the evangelist and his readers back into the life of Jesus. As just noted, this tendency is particularly evident in the Fourth Gospel. In this Gospel we encounter a profusion of references to Jewish attempts to kill or arrest Jesus. As early as chapter 5, the fact that Jesus had cured a man at the pool of Bethesda on the Sabbath and made claims for his own identity suggesting an equality with God, induced the Jews to attempt to kill him (5.18). On a number of occasions Jesus reminded them that they would seek to kill him (7.19, 8.37, 8.40 and 8.44) and he even tried to avoid Judaea because of their attitude (7.1). Twice in the Gospel there are actually attempts made to stone him (8.59

and 10.31). His disciples raise the possibility of his being stoned as a reason for not visiting Lazarus (11.8). The high priests even planned to kill Lazarus because many believed in Jesus on account of him (12.10–11). There are also several references to attempts to apprehend Jesus prior to the arrest which leads to his crucifixion (7.30, 7.32, 7.44, 8.20, 10.39 and 11.57).

The extent of this material, which indicates a violent Jewish antipathy to Jesus, is best explained not on the basis of the experience of the historical Jesus but as reflecting extremely poor relations between the Johannine community and the Jews with whom it was in contact. John even works into his Gospel a statement in which Jesus suggests his position in this regard would later be paralleled by that of his disciples: 'If the world hates you, know that it has hated me before it hated you' (15.18). In this context 'hate' is a word which, in sociological terms, indicates that a sectarian cleavage has opened up between John's community and Judaism. The Johannine Jesus, after all, told his disciples at the Last Supper: 'You will be expelled from the synagogue' (16.2). This remark functions to legitimate the sectarian status of his community *vis-à-vis* Judaism by suggesting that it is a reality which Jesus himself had predicted would occur. Yet the yawning division between the two groups is even more apparent when one considers the manner in which the figure of Abraham is treated in John's Gospel.

According to Genesis 15–17, Abraham was the physical progenitor of the Jewish people, the person through whom God gave that people its homeland, the founder of its religion and the outstanding exemplar of its faith. First-century Jews were proud of their lineage from Abraham. They were prone to say 'we have Abraham as our father' (Matt. 3.9; Luke 3.8). Underlying such an attitude was the sense of identity which came from sharing a single ancestor. But also significant, as I explained in Chapter 2, was that in this culture honour was regarded as the primary virtue and ascribed honour came to those who were born into an honourable family. For this reason all Jews basked in the honour of their illustrious ancestor Abraham. At a theological level, moreover, descendants of Abraham and his son Isaac were parties to the covenant which Yahweh had made with his people. In Gen. 17.19 Yahweh says to Abraham: 'Sarah your wife shall bear you a son, and you shall call his name Isaac. I will establish my covenant with him as an everlasting covenant for his descendants after him.'

The sign and seal of being a member of the covenant people was circumcision (Gen. 17.9–14).

As the various communities which acknowledged Jesus as Messiah set off on the journeys which would eventually separate them from Judaism, the figure of Abraham posed a considerable problem. In Galatia, for example, it is clear that those who were disturbing Paul's Gentile converts had made a powerful case for the necessity of becoming a descendant of Abraham, through circumcision, to enjoy the benefits of God's covenant with him. The New Testament reveals a variety of ways in which the followers of Jesus responded to the challenge posed to their identity by the Jewish claim to descent in blood and in faith from Abraham. One response was to seek to enlist Abraham as a progenitor of the new movement, a strategy adopted in Paul's rather artificial argument in Galatians 3. Similarly, both Matthew (1.2) and Luke (3.34) manage to list Abraham as an ancestor of Jesus in their respective genealogies.

Yet the response of the Fourth Evangelist to the question of Abraham, which is found entirely within the confines of 8.31–59, is utterly different. The fundamental organising principle of this part of John's Gospel consists of a series of Jewish objections to what Jesus says, matched with his responses. The foundation of this pattern lies in the typically Mediterranean cultural feature of a contest for honour to be obtained from the social interaction of challenge and response described in Chapter 2. John 8.31–59 begins as follows: 'Then Jesus began to speak to the Jews who had believed him, "If you remain in my word, you are truly my disciples and you will know the truth and the truth will set you free"' (8.31–2; my translation). The frequency with which this saying of Jesus is repeated, in contemporary Christian circles, out of the context and as an expression of piety, may disguise the sharpness of the point it is making. What Jesus has said actually constitutes an ambiguous challenge (see Chapter 2) to his Jewish audience. At one level it is an exalted assertion of theological truth, yet in its cultural context it conveys a possible reproach, namely, that these Jews are not already free, and this is exactly how they interpret it: 'They answered him, "We are the descendants of Abraham, and have never been in bondage to anyone. How is it that you say, 'You will be made free'?"' (8.33). Jesus vigorously responds to this challenge (8.34–8) and to each of the six subsequent challenges the Jews make to him (8.39, 41, 48, 52,

57 and 59). The whole passage constitutes an unbroken exchange from the lofty and *prima facie* abstract theological generality of vv.31–2 to the attempt to stone Jesus in v.59. By the power of his argumentation and his escape from them in v.59 Jesus defends and vindicates his honour. Accordingly, John 8.31–59 makes excellent sense as an extended example of challenge and response. This observation, however, hardly exhausts the meaning of the passage. As I have already noted in Chapter 1, although anthropology exposes the basic social script of this culture, it does not necessarily help us understand the precise configurations of any particular interaction. Further investigation of this passage is assisted by reference to Bryan Wilson's introversionist response.

What we find in John 8.31–59 is a progressive reduction in the significance of Abraham within the scheme of salvation. In the first and second sections of the controversy (8.31–8 and 8.39–41) Jesus is faced with the Jewish claim to descent from Abraham as a riposte to the suggestion of their unfreedom implied in the saying 'the truth will set you free'. Jesus' answer is to deny that they are truly Abraham's descendants because they seek to kill him, which is not the way Abraham acted. The Johannine Jesus, however, does not follow the route taken in other parts of the New Testament by claiming for himself or his followers Abrahamic descent in place of the Jews. After the next two sections (8.41–47 and 8.48–51), in which the trading of insults reaches a new intensity, Abraham again enters the discussion. In 8.52-6 Jesus, in effect, responds affirmatively to the question that he is greater than Abraham by saying: 'Your father Abraham rejoiced that he was to see my day; he saw it and was glad' (8.56). The basis for this assertion is a Jewish tradition, most clearly expressed in the *Apocalypse of Abraham* (to be dated to the period 70–120 CE), in which Abraham is given a vision of the End which actually includes the feature that in that period God would send his chosen one to summon his people (*Apocalypse of Abraham* 29.14–31; and chapters 30 and 31). Yet the fact that in John 8.56 Jesus asserts that Abraham would see his (Jesus') day suggests that in John's time there existed a tradition wherein the notion of Abraham's eschatological vision had been given a Christian twist, namely, by reinterpreting the 'chosen one' or similar eschatological agent to mean Jesus himself. There is actually evidence for such a Christianised version of this particular tradition in that part of the *Apocalypse of Abraham* which is widely regarded as a

Christian interpolation (29.3–13). Plainly enough, such a version could only have originated among Christians who, like Paul, desired to maintain a place for Abraham in the ideology of the new movement.

But this is not John's way. In the penultimate section of the controversy Jesus says to his Jewish audience: 'Truly, truly, I say to you, before Abraham was, I am' (8.58). By this remark the Johannine Jesus enunciates a claim to an identity which is exalted far above that of Abraham. It is virtually a claim to divine status. Not unnaturally, it provokes the Jews to attempt to stone him, presumably for blasphemy. It would be a mistake, however, to see in this statement merely an example of the high Christology of the Fourth Gospel. In social terms, Jesus has depicted Abraham as utterly insignificant beside himself and, by necessary implication, treated claims to Abrahamic descent as nothing in comparison with faith in him. The Johannine Jesus is suggesting that Abraham is irrelevant to the Christian community. This attitude, completely at odds with Paul's approach, indicates, by the fact that John's community had turned their back on a central aspect of Jewish tradition, how socially isolated they had become from Judaism. In this respect their response to the world is a powerfully introversionist one.

When we turn to John's views on salvation, it should be noted initially that like every New Testament author he had to cope with the fact that in Jesus a new era of salvation had been inaugurated, that there had been an irruption of God into the world, yet the end of the process was still to occur. Although John refers to both the present and the future perspectives – for example in the striking expression which he uses twice: 'the hour is coming, and now is' (4.23 and 5.25) – he emphasises the notion of salvation in the present more than other New Testament authors. He has been described as favouring 'realised eschatology' (Ashton 1986: 10–11 and 1991: 220–6). In this respect his outlook has introversionist overtones. Thus he repeatedly introduces the idea that 'eternal life' is available to believers here and now: 'Truly, truly, I say to you, the person who hears my words and believes the one who sent me has eternal life, and does not come into judgement but has passed from death to life' (5.24; my translation). On another occasion he says simply 'the one who believes has eternal life' (6.47). It is this element which seems to predominate in John.

Although he does include some indications of a futurist eschatology so common in the Synoptics, especially references to resurrection or judgement 'on the last day' (5.28–9; 6.39, 6.40, 6.44, 6.51c–8 and 12.48), the text exhibits little, if any, interest in when this last day will occur or what will characterise it. It is certainly not presented as imminent. The Johannine community, therefore, can be regarded as introversionist in its preoccupation with its own holiness and in its belief that only through belonging to it and believing in Jesus Christ can salvation come.

EPILOGUE: THE QUESTION OF DUALISM

We return to the question of dualism in the Community Rule and the Fourth Gospel with which we began this chapter. Two existing explanations should be mentioned. First, there is an article by James H. Charlesworth, in which the author points to a number of expressions found in one part of the Community Rule (1QS 3.13–4.26) which have close parallels in John and argues that the explanation for these correspondences lies in Johannine traditions having been directly influenced by Qumran terminology in Palestine (1990: 76–106). More recently, John Ashton, who also points to similar dualistic contrasts in Qumran and in John between, for example, truth and falsehood, and the community and the outside world, has gone further than Charlesworth by tentatively proposing that the Fourth Evangelist himself may well have started life as one of the Essenes who were to be found, according to Josephus, in large numbers in every town in Palestine (*Jewish War* II.124) (1991: 237). One problem with this view is that there is no great dualism in CD, which does seem to be connected with the Essenes scattered in communities throughout Palestine, while there is in 1QS, which relates to a desert community.

In the space available I am unable thoroughly to canvas the viewpoints of Charlesworth and Ashton. Nevertheless, there does seem to be another explanation for the existence of dualism in the Fourth Gospel and in 1QS. As we have seen, the introversionist nature of the two communities was manifested in a profound separation between members and non-members, the community and the world. Dualism at the level of ideology and symbolism is plausibly to be explained as an inevitable reflection of the fact that the fundamental social reality for both groups was a marked division between themselves and the outside world. In such a context, dualism comes naturally. That is to say, the communities for whom these two texts were written both exhibited, although in very different ways, a form of sectarianism which was powerfully introversionist and which, feeding on similar scriptural and even cultural traditions, produced dualistic outlooks having some elements in common.

Chapter 6

Millennialism and Daniel 7

THE TRADITION OF THE FOURTH BEAST

At the start of Daniel 7 the seer recounts a night vision he had of four beasts which rose from the depths of the Great Sea. The first beast was like a lion and had eagle's wings, the second was like a bear, and the third like a leopard with four birds' wings and four heads. The fourth beast, however, was worse than any of these. It was 'fearsome and grisly and exceedingly strong, with great iron teeth. It devoured and crunched, and it trampled underfoot what was left. It was different from all the beasts which went before it, and had ten horns' (7.7; REB). As the seer was considering the horns, another horn, a small one, appeared among the others and three of the original horns were uprooted to make way for it. 'In this horn were eyes like human eyes and a mouth that uttered bombast' (7.8; REB). As the seer looks on, the heavenly court abruptly appears and the beast is killed and its carcass consigned to the flames (7.9–12). There follows the celebrated description of the arrival of one like a human being (literally 'like a son of man' – *kevar enosh* in the Aramaic), to whom are given sovereignty and glory and kingly power (7.13–14).

Troubled and dismayed, Daniel seeks guidance as to the meaning of what he has seen from one of those present. He is told: 'These great beasts, four in number, are four kingdoms which will arise from the earth. But the holy ones of the Most High will receive the kingly power and retain possession of it always, for ever and ever' (7.17–18). Daniel then seeks a more detailed explanation, since he sees the horn waging war against 'the holy ones' with some success, until the arrival of the Ancient in Years and the award of judgement in their favour, together with kingly power. His heavenly informant then obliges him with a long interpretation in which he mentions that the last horn, in its campaign against 'the holy ones of the Most High', will try to alter festival seasons and religious laws. But eventually it will be destroyed and kingly power, sovereignty and greatness of all the kingdoms under heaven will be given to the holy people of the Most High (7.19–27).

Although we should reject one-on-one interpretations of religious symbolism (because they involve misreading complexes of meaning as mere ciphers), there can be little doubt that the fourth beast, the fourth kingdom, is a broad reference to the Greeks, to the Seleucid Kingdom of Syria in particular, and that the last horn refers to Antiochus IV Epiphanes, who in the period 167–164 BCE sought, perhaps with some local help, to control if not destroy the traditional Judaism of the Law and the Temple. He was ultimately foiled in this enterprise by an uprising led by the Maccabean family. Daniel 7 is to be dated to this period, perhaps the early part, between the profanation of the Temple in 167 BCE and its reconsecration by Judas Maccabeus in 164 BCE. I interpret the holy ones of the Most High, and, indeed, the figure described as one like a human being, as the suffering Israelites and not, as in some interpretations, the angels. What we find in this vision, therefore, is the use of the apocalyptic genre, at a time of the imposition of brute political and religious oppression upon Israel, to identify and denigrate the oppressor and to foretell his coming destruction and the glorious vindication of those whom he has oppressed.

Let us now travel some 250 years onwards. We come to another apocalyptic work, 4 Ezra, which was written around 100 CE in the aftermath of the Roman conquest of Israel and the destruction of Jerusalem, the savagery of which not even the Jewish historian Josephus, with his eyes ever on his Flavian patrons, could obscure when he wrote of these events in *The Jewish War*. For the author of 4 Ezra the destruction of Israel which had been threatening under Antiochus has become real. The feature of this work most germane to our purpose is that here, too, we find the image of the fourth beast. For in the famous vision of chapter 11 an eagle is roused roaring from the sea and is addressed by a lion (a messianic figure) as follows:

Are you not the one that remains of the four beasts which I had made to reign in my world, so that the end of the times might come through them? You, the fourth that has come, have

> conquered all the beasts that have gone before; and you have
> held sway over the earth with much terror, and over all the
> earth with grievous oppression . . . you have destroyed the
> fortifications of those who brought forth fruit, and have laid
> low the walls of those who did you no harm. And so your
> insolence has come up before the Most High . . . Therefore,
> you will surely disappear, you eagle.
>
> (11.39–45; Stone 1990: 344–5)

Ezra seeks an interpretation and is told: 'The eagle which you saw
coming up from the sea is the fourth kingdom which appeared in
a vision to your brother Daniel. But it was not explained to him as I
now explain it to you' (12.11; Stone 1990: 358). Once again,
although religious symbolism is never exhausted by pointing to
one referent, it is reasonably clear that in the eagle the power and
arrogance of Rome are manifested and its destruction foretold.

The third work which we must consider, also from around the
end of the first century CE (Collins 1984: 54–83), is the last book in
the New Testament, the Apocalypse. Like Daniel, John also had a
vision:

> Then I saw a beast rising out of the sea. It had ten horns and
> seven heads; on the horns were ten diadems, and on each
> diadem was a blasphemous name. The beast I saw resembled a
> leopard, but its feet were like a bear's and its mouth like a lion's.
> The dragon conferred on it his own power, his throne, and
> great authority.
>
> (13.1–2; *REB*)

A little later the seer describes how 'the beast was allowed to
mouth bombast and blasphemy' (13.5; REB) and 'was also allowed
to wage war on God's people and defeat them, and it was given
authority over every tribe, nation, language, and race' (13.7;
REB).

The allusions to the beasts of Daniel 7 in the verses first quoted
are unmistakable. The author has created a composite monster
which incorporates all the features of the four Danielic beasts,
although in reverse order. Pride of place goes to the ten horns
from the fourth beast, the resemblance to the leopard evokes the
third beast, the bear's feet the second and the lion's mouth the
first. That the beast utters bombast and makes war against the
holy ones is strongly reminiscent of the activities of the little horn
in Daniel 7, where the reference is to Antiochus IV Epiphanes

and his assault on the Jews in 167–164 BCE. A reading of these verses and other parts of the Apocalypse makes it clear that Rome is the primary referent of the beast, although, here too, it is a grave interpretative error to suppose that such an identification in any way exhausts its richly evocative meaning.

The motif of the seven heads in 13.1 is much older than Daniel, however. This feature can be seen in Lotan, the seven-headed serpent referred to in Ugaritic myth (*The Palace of Baal* vv.38–9), which seems to be identical with Leviathan (a monster, along with Rahab, defeated by Yahweh – Job 9.13; Ps. 74.13–14, where Leviathan's heads are mentioned, and 89.10; Isa. 27.1 and 51.9) and has even older antecedents as Ti'amat, the salt-water abyss defeated by Marduk in the Babylonian Enuma Elish saga. It may be that the notion of a composite beast owes something to the statues, part human and part animal, known to us from Mesopotamia. In one powerful image the author fuses the tradition of the primordial sea-monster and the explicitly political beasts described in Daniel 7 to say something about Rome and its power.

In these three works, therefore, we observe a literary tradition stretching across 250 years which relates the imagery of beasts presented in the apocalyptic genre to the harsh realities of political domination. In particular, the fourth beast is employed as an image or symbol of such oppression, expressly in the case of Daniel and 4 Ezra and by implication in the Apocalypse. The significance of these interconnections obviously makes this a rich field for a literary study focusing on the question of intertextuality. In this book, however, we are pursuing a social-scientific approach. An application of ideas from sociology and anthropology to the use of fourth beast imagery in these three works prompts a range of questions, for example, as to the nature of the apocalyptic genre, as to the role of mythopoesis in such a context, where the myth being created relates to the future and not the past, and, perhaps most fundamentally, as to the social function of treating political oppression in an apocalypse. To fire the sociological imagination on these questions, we must look to social-scientific writings which deal with contemporary phenomena that are at least roughly comparable with the Jewish and Christian experience and cover both perspectives on the fourth beast, first, as a power threatening to devastate Israel (Daniel) and, secondly, as one which has already done so (4 Ezra). In the current chapter I will deal with Daniel 7, in the next chapter with 4 Ezra and in Chapter 8 with the Apocalypse. Although my own research in this area began with the Apocalypse, it soon became clear that to come to grips with the political issues in that text it was necessary to consider other Jewish apocalyptic works which treat of oppression by foreign powers. As I will argue in the last chapter, however, the Apocalypse actually diverges from the Jewish texts, since although it demonises Rome, it does so in a context where the Roman Empire was not persecuting the Christian communities. This phenomenon will require the presentation of quite a different hypothesis to explain its anti-Roman mythopoesis.

THE APOCALYPTIC GENRE IN SOCIAL-SCIENTIFIC PERSPECTIVE

The place to go for this comparative material is the abundant research which has been conducted into the impact of colonial powers on indigenous peoples and their social and religious systems. Such interaction frequently leads to the development of religious movements with a millennial (or 'revolutionist') orientation which look forward to the dramatic transformation of this world, the destruction of the white oppressor and the restoration of ancestral ways and even of the ancestors themselves. The cargo cults of the South Pacific are the most well-known examples, although comparable phenomena have occurred in Africa and North America. Helpful treatments of such material have been written by Burridge (1969), Worsley (1970) and Wilson (1975). With one or two exceptions (Isenberg 1974; Reid 1989), there has been a surprising failure to apply these social-scientific perspectives to the study of Jewish apocalypses, even though this material has been utilised in a number of studies into Hebrew prophecy (Overholt 1986). Lester L. Grabbe has written a useful prolegomenon to the application of the social sciences to apocalyptic literature (1989), but unfortunately adopts the questionable position that more work remains to be done on the social-scientific side before the enterprise can really get under way.

In adopting this approach, we do not prescind from the results of recent research by biblical critics which has done much to clarify the meanings of 'apocalypse' and 'apocalyptic'. It has become clear in recent years that the preferable course is to regard apocalypse as a Jewish literary genre (Collins 1978), the original and central interests of which lay in its relating direct revelation from God or an angel concerning heavenly mysteries and speculative interests, such as cosmology, astronomy and the calendar (Stone 1976). This line of attack does more justice to the origins and nature of extant apocalyptic literature than the older perspective on the genre as a mode of expressing a social or religious phenomenon, which theologians often call apocalypticism but which social scientists usually refer to as millennialism, and which involved such elements as an expectation of 'the world's last day', cosmic catastrophe, a division of time into particular ages, messianic figures and salvation for the chosen beyond the catastrophe (Koch 1972: 28–33). Since some apocalypses, like Greek Baruch, do not exhibit 'apocalypticism' of this sort, while some of its elements appear in non-apocalyptic works, such as the Testaments of the Twelve Patriarchs (Stone 1976: 440), it is probably best to eschew the use of 'apocalypticism' altogether and replace it with 'millennialism' or 'millenarianism' or something similar (such as Wilson's 'revolutionist response'). Having said this, it should not be forgotten that even apocalypses which focus on issues like the calendar (such as 1 Enoch 72–82) may well have a political aspect, not only because the calendar may be tied to the proper administration of the lucrative Temple cult, but for the more general reason that control over the way that time is structured is often a medium of hierarchic power and governance (Munn 1992: 109).

As a consequence of this shift of direction, the issue of the social location of apocalyptic writings has inevitably become a more difficult one. Nevertheless, the use of the fourth beast as emblematic of political oppression in works as far apart in time as Daniel 7 and 4 Ezra underlines the fact that in the apocalyptic writings there are some which do reflect a context in the type of social and religious conditions which scholars of an older generation described as 'apocalypticism'. E.P. Sanders (1989) has recently pointed to the following works in this connection: first, from the period 167–164 BCE we have, in addition to Daniel 7, certain other visions in Daniel 7–12, the Animal Apocalypse in 1 Enoch 83–90 and Jubilees 23; and, secondly, in the post-70 CE period we have 2 Baruch, the Apocalypse of Abraham and the Testament of Levi, in addition to 4 Ezra. Sanders rightly regards these works, a significant part of the apocalyptic corpus, as having in common the fact that they exhibit 'in revelation' feelings of oppression and hopes for the restoration of Israel.

It is not entirely surprising that the apocalyptic genre, which had developed under the influence of, if not directly out of, wisdom and mantic traditions and whose core was the revelation of divine mysteries, should come to be employed by Israelite scribes at times of national distress and oppression, especially when the actions of imperial powers put difficulties of one kind or another in the way of access to the two central Jewish redemptive media, the Law and the Temple. In such situations the apocalyptic tradition offered a direct mode of access to God and the divine intention for Israel and her foes which could stand in substitution for the Temple or the Law. In Chapter 8 we will see that rather different factors are at work in the Apocalypse. We shall now proceed to the modern comparative material.

SOCIAL-SCIENTIFIC PERSPECTIVES: MILLENARIANISM, COGNITIVE DISSONANCE AND INTROVERSIONISM

The history of Africa, America, Australia and New Zealand in the last two centuries provides many examples of the results of confrontation between an indigenous society with its own cultural and religious traditions and a colonial power. From the ancient period, we may cite the Greek and then Roman conquest of many native peoples around the Mediterranean, including the inhabitants of Palestine. The interaction between colonial power and local people will often climax with the unequivocal imposition of its authority by the invader. This result is frequently accomplished by the infliction upon the local people of some notable calamity, such as a disastrous military defeat. Sometimes, on the other hand, the lifestyle and institutions of the local people are weakened or even destroyed without any single climactic event, simply through the debilitating exposure to a more technologically advanced civilisation.

The attitudes of the indigenous people to the colonising power tend to be quite different depending upon whether they are expressed before or after a watershed event in the relationship or the final realisation that their culture has been irremediably harmed by the interaction. Before such an event or realisation, a millenarian or, to use Bryan Wilson's term, a 'revolutionist' outlook often prevails. That is to say, the local people passionately hope for some imminent, supernatural transformation of the current situation, especially through the destruction of the invading force and the restoration of their traditional lands, lifestyle and beliefs. Often the millennial dream will refer to their reacquisition of political power. It is very common for one particular person, usually with charismatic gifts, to articulate the discontent of his or her people and to shape the vision of the coming restoration of their fortunes. Such a leader may even co-ordinate military action against the invader and is frequently the focus of messianic expectations. After the almost inevitable calamity, which will frequently represent a profound disappointment of millennial expectations, radical changes in attitude tend to occur. At first there may be a period of what social scientists call 'cognitive dissonance' (Festinger 1957), in this case the agonising sense of discrepancy between the hope of the native people for vindication and the actual course of events. Since there is often, although not always, a strong human compulsion to reduce such dissonance, the experience frequently produces a change of outlook. Faced with the harsh realities of defeat, or even the less traumatic dissolution of traditional lifestyle, those who have been vanquished or profoundly disorientated generally give up the prospect of reacquiring political power and may exhibit various forms of introversionist response to the world, by adopting strategies of voluntary withdrawal, either social or even geographical. This entire progression can be seen, for example, in seventeenth-century England, which witnessed the transition from movements exhibiting various forms of millennial belief, through the disappointment caused by the restoration of the monarchy in 1660, to the emergence of introversionist groups thereafter (Hill 1985; Rowland 1988: 89–114). My focus in this chapter is on the first phase of this progression – the millennial or revolutionist one in so far as it assists in understanding Daniel. In the next chapter I will deal with the subsequent stages – cognitive dissonance and introversionism – in the context of an investigation of the social function of 4 Ezra.

At the most fundamental level, revolutionist movements express dissatisfaction with prevailing political, social, economic or religious conditions and look forward to their radical and supernatural transformation and replacement by an entirely new order. Movements usually classified as millenarian include the wide variety of medieval phenomena studied by Norman Cohn (Cohn 1970), the Diggers and other seventeenth-century English groups, and modern examples, such as the Jehovah's witnesses. They are typified most dramatically, however, in the numerous cargo cults of Melanesia and certain other religious movements in the South Pacific, which have been analysed by Kenelm Burridge, Peter Worsley and others. Other examples can be found among the native peoples of North and South America. I will deal with three examples in a moment.

Millenarian movements of the type soon to be mentioned have occurred in situations where colonial regimes have suppressed local cultures or disturbed their inner dynamics, leading to various types of absolute or relative deprivation. 'Absolute deprivation' refers to the actual removal of various goods from the subject group, while 'relative deprivation' means 'a negative discrepancy between legitimate expectation and actuality' (Aberle 1970: 209). I do not for a moment suggest, however, that deprivation can itself provide an explanation for the creation of a millenarian movement, since at times deprivation does not produce millenarianism, while on other, generally rare, occasions millenarianism seems to occur in its absence. An example of this is set out below. Rather, the preferable view is that deprivation is sometimes a factor in a particular example and that in such a case the nature of deprivation or oppression existing at the time of the writing of the text must be examined in order to understand its symbolism and the ideology of the movement for which it was composed.

One further point should be made before moving to the modern examples. The future expectation of these movements is generally formulated as a sacred narrative which recounts how the existing order will be destroyed and replaced with a 'new heaven and a new earth'. The creation of such a narrative or 'myth', as we may properly describe it, constitutes the most potent point of comparison between modern millenarian movements and the vision in Daniel 7. In taking this view we must shed the negative attitudes to myth which have been so prevalent in the field even before Bultmann's programme of demythologisation. Bultmann was under a misapprehension springing from nineteenth-century rationalist ideas that myth was a form of primitive science (Bultmann 1964: 3–5). In this century anthropologists have amply documented a range of vital social functions fulfilled by myth. Thus, functionalists such as Malinowski stressed the ways in which myths contributed to the preservation of social stability (Malinowski 1948). With the reaction against the static bias of functionalist analysis and the movement towards more change- and conflict-oriented social models, our understanding of myth has developed to encompass situations in which it serves to stress the goal rather than the basis of a social order. A lingering consequence of the functionalist approach has been a failure to appreciate the significance of myths which speak of future events. It is precisely in the context of millennial movements that we find myths dealing with the future, because they arise in the midst of societies going through crisis or at least great change where current mythic self-understandings are out of phase with the social situation, as may be seen in the first of our two examples.

THREE EXAMPLES OF MILLENNIALISM

The Vailala madness

In 1919 a religious movement began in the neighbourhood of Vailala in the Gulf Division of Papua which came to be called the Vailala madness, because of the various types of dissociative state manifested by those involved. One pidgin-English description for this phenomenon was 'head-he-go-round'. The movement was characterised by much ecstatic behaviour both collective and individual, as well as by a set of beliefs and an elementary ritual. These beliefs were expressed in the form of a simple myth. The ancestors of the members of the movement were soon to return to them. They were expected in a large steamer, which was to be loaded with 'cargo' – cases of gifts such as tobacco, calico, knives, axes and foodstuffs (Williams 1976: 341). Some early versions of the myth specified that the steamer was to contain a consignment of rifles which would be used in driving the whites out of Papua (342). In some places, moreover, the returning ancestors were expected to be white. In anticipation of the arrival of the steamer, many sacred objects from local cults were destroyed and some groups ceased to practise agriculture and hunting and gathering. Mortuary feasts were instituted in anticipation of the arrival of the ancestors.

F.E. Williams, an Australian Government anthropologist who observed the movement in its latter stages, actually came across two objects which seem to have contributed much to the myth. Some natives had alleged that Evara, a founder of the movement, had in his possession papers which had come fluttering out of the sky. The reality was somewhat different. Evara did possess a modern novel entitled *Love and the Aeroplane*, on the cover of which was a picture of a man and a woman precariously attached to the plane by a rope (1976: 353). The other object which Evara possessed was an advertisement for Lifebuoy Soap, depicting a field-hospital, a motor-ambulance and a number of figures in uniform. Evara explained that one of the minor figures in the advertisement was himself and that rest were his deceased relatives. Accordingly, while the movement was actually engaged in mythopoesis, it did have a few prompts from white civilisation (Schwimmer 1976: 40).

In time the movement waned. The failure of the expected events produced divergent reactions. In later years many came to believe that the steamer of the dead had actually arrived – it had been clearly heard and dimly seen. In other cases, persons claiming miraculous attributes were exposed as rank impostors (Williams 1976: 383–95). To recent researchers (although not to Williams himself) it is clear that the movement was a response to white intervention in native affairs, through missionary efforts and mining activities. It 'expressed powerful native resentment at their social and political position in the new order of things' (Worsley 1970: 89).

The Ghost Dance

Our second example, the phenomenon known as the Ghost Dance, represents the last flame of resistance by North American Indians against white conquest. There were actually two Ghost Dances, the first in 1870 and the second in 1890. The first originated with a Paiute Indian from Nevada whose name was Tävibo ('White Man'). He had visions and was reputed to be invulnerable to bullets, a quite common belief among indigenous peoples seeking to combat white colonisation. His initial message, gained from communing with the Great Spirit on a mountain top, was that there was soon to be a devastating earthquake which would swallow up all whites, leaving behind, however, their houses, goods and stores. Later he announced that both Indians and whites would be engulfed but that after three days the Indians and all the game would return, though the whites would be gone forever. Still later he claimed that only Indians who believed his message would be saved. The story he told, which is a futurist myth, was actually enacted in the form of a dance, in a circle around a central fire (La Barre 1978: 227–9).

The second Ghost Dance, of 1890, was led by one Wovoka, also a Paiute, and alleged to be the son of Tävibo. His message, performed in a dance, was that there was soon to be a great earthquake which would signal his arrival as messiah to inaugurate the new world and the return of the dead ancestors. This dance caused a wave of excitement among a number of tribes. Many developed somewhat different versions of the same myth, although most believed that the whites would be destroyed by supernatural means. Unfortunately, the Sioux, the largest and strongest tribe in the United States, resorted to bringing on the millennium by naturalistic means, namely armed revolt. This led to conflict with white troops and the tragedy of the Battle of Wounded Knee in December 1890, when 200 Indians – men, women and children – were killed with Hotchkiss guns. Never again did a considerable body of Indians in North America seek to threaten their new masters (La Barre 1978: 229–32).

The very similar myths generated and enacted in the Ghost Dances contained a belief in a new heaven on earth and the miraculous reappearance of dead ancestors and the old tribal ways of life. They clearly reflected, in the terms of Bryan Wilson's typology, a revolutionist response to the disintegration of Indian culture under the pressure of an ever advancing white frontier (La Barre 1978: 144).

The migration of the Tupi-Guarani

In precolonial Brazil there occurred a millennial movement which does not appear to have been based on any form of deprivation (see the discussion in Ribeiro 1970). Prior to Portuguese conquest a number of mass migrations took place among the Tupi-Guarani tribes, at first from the interior to coastal regions and later also along the coast northwards. Underlying these migrations was a myth of two creations. The first world had been destroyed by flood, but a number of its inhabitants, heroic figures who had practised virtuous behaviour, had been able to escape destruction by joining the Creator in his abode. So too the present world was to be destroyed and its inhabitants would only escape if, having perfected themselves, they travelled to join God in his abode, the Land without Evil, which lay to the east at the end of a long and difficult journey. It appears that occasionally a prophet would arise among the Tupi-Guarani, reveal that the end of the world was imminent and promise to lead them to the Land without Evil, their paradise. The migrations seem to have been triggered by such prophecy, and not, as far as we know, by population pressure, war, disease or other forms of deprivation. Later, however, there were examples of Indian migrations to the Land without Evil stimulated by the disturbances brought by Portuguese conquest or missionary activity, in which case an existing futurist myth was being re-employed in the more usual context of deprivation. This phenomenon, at least in its pre-colonial phase, represents, therefore, the rare case of a millennial movement with profound practical consequences brought into existence around an existing futurist myth for reasons which were primarily religious. It provides a cautionary tale against assuming that a millennial movement always presupposes absolute or relative deprivation.

DANIEL 7 IN SOCIAL-SCIENTIFIC PERSPECTIVE

A considerable body of evidence exists as to the course of events in Palestine in 167–164 BCE outside of the confines of Daniel. Much of this is to be found in Jewish sources, such as 1 and 2 Maccabees, although there is also some non-Jewish material. There are many ways of interpreting the onslaught on Judaism which occurred during this period and the most important of them have been discussed recently by Daniel Harrington (1988: 92–7). Thus, Elias Bickerman saw it as a civil war of an essentially religious character which had as its most serious consequence the defiling of the Temple. Viktor Tcherikover regarded it as a clash between wealthy Hellenising interests in Jerusalem, supported by the Seleucids, and the common people, while Klaus Bringman argued that it was the result of Antiochus IV seeking to consolidate his own power and the income which flowed to him from Israel. Whatever position one adopts, there can be little doubt that a considerable segment of the Jewish population was subjected to gross oppression in various forms, ranging from the profanation of the Temple, which led to the discontinuance of Yahwist worship there, to a widespread ban on adherence to the Law, with the most severe penalties being inflicted on those who refused to abandon their beliefs and practices. The edict of Antiochus referred to in 1 Macc. 1.41 seems to reflect the historical reality that he did actively seek to extirpate much of Jewish religion.

The drastic nature of the deprivation suffered by many Israelites during the period 167–164 BCE at the hands of a foreign ruler leads naturally to a comparison with the social-scientific material just mentioned. The events of this period are readily explicable in terms of a drastic readjustment of various forms of power operative in Israel, including the political and military power of a foreign monarch (which could extend to proscribing the practice of traditional Jewish religion), the power over the cult wielded by the high priest and the economic power represented by the wealth stored in the Temple and by the ability to extract tribute from the populace. Yet the religious significance of such events should not be forgotten. As Kenelm Burridge has observed in the South Pacific context (1969: 4–6), religion is concerned with sources of power which are regarded as particularly creative or destructive. In particular, in a religious context spiritual beings become identified as a source or principle of power having certain defined attributes. Religion, in fact, by allowing access to and interaction with such beings, is actually concerned with the systematic reordering of different kinds of power. Every society develops a system of rules for dealing with and appropriating such power. These rules have as their counterparts a system of obligations which are communal and individual. Such obligations must be discharged and the 'process whereby individuals attempt to discharge their obligations in relation to the moral imperatives of the community is no less than a redemptive process' (Burridge 1969: 6).

Sheldon R. Isenberg, who has sought to apply the insights of Burridge to Judaism in general and the Qumran community during the first century CE in particular, has interpreted Burridge on this point as follows:

> The total discharge of debts so that there is no more obligedness is one way of talking about salvation or redemption. If a society is so structured that individuals or a group perceive themselves to be systematically and structurally denied access

to the redemptive media, if they seem to be blocked from discharging their debts and are thus deprived of the possibility of fulfilling their human potentialities, then serious problems arise.

(1974: 29)

The basic redemptive media were the individual and group fulfilment of the requirements of the Torah and the related but institutionally distinguishable sacrificial system. A Jew achieved redemption, in the sense explained above, by adherence to the Law and participation in the Temple cult. The action taken by Antiochus and possibly some Hellenising Jews in the period in question constituted a direct and violent attack on both of these principal redemptive media. This danger was, if anything, even more extreme than that faced by modern indigenous peoples and the movements that have arisen among them, where problems have been caused more through the disturbance of traditional roles and values by exposure to an apparently superior European civilisation, even in the absence of efforts by local administrators to suppress local culture, than by the direct exercise of force.

As already noted, deprivation of this sort does not always lead to millenarianism; its mere occurrence is an entirely insufficient basis for predicting whether a people affected by it will attempt to overcome it and, if they do so, whether they will try to change the situation, transcend it or simply withdraw from it. In the Jewish response to the events of 167–64 BCE we observe a variety of responses. The most effective one was the armed rebellion led by the Maccabees. Parallels to this type of reaction exist in the armed struggles by indigenous peoples against disturbances to traditional patterns, especially as to land ownership, brought about by white colonisation; one example is the Maori Hau Hau movement of the 1860s. Another response to the Seleucid onslaught came from a group called the Hasideans. These seem to have been scribes (1 Macc. 7.12–13) in Israel who were separate from the Maccabees but allied themselves with them (1 Macc. 2.42).

Daniel 7 consists of a visionary narrative of future events, akin to the millennial myths found in modern religious movements, such as the Vailala madness and the Ghost Dance of the North American Indians, describing the appearance and career of evocative animals and horns and their attack on certain 'holy ones' and culminating in their eventual defeat accompanied by the vindication of those holy ones. To appreciate in more detail how such an account may be examined using the social-scientific perspectives set out above, we must attend to its literary form. In chapter 7 we find the pattern of a dream vision which relates mysterious events metaphorically, followed by their interpretation in terms of natural human experience offered by a divinely aided figure. The same pattern is also found in Daniel 2 and 4, of Nebuchadnezzar's dreams of the statue and the tree respectively, which are interpreted for him by Daniel. We obtain guidance in how to interpret the same pattern in Daniel 7 by analogy with these earlier chapters and by considering how metaphor works.

As already noted, one-on-one interpretation of the figures in Daniel 7 (such as proposed by Di Lella 1977) should be resisted. It is clear that we are not dealing with a code simply requiring translation, since many details in the visionary sections are not touched on at all or only very briefly (for example, the sea or the attributes of the first three beasts). More fundamentally, however, as Max Black has argued (Black 1962 and 1979; applied to Daniel by Porter 1983), metaphor simply does not function in this way. Metaphor does not offer a substitute for one thing ('the primary object'), but rather connects the primary object with a web or system of meaning ('the secondary object') which has the effect of altering our perception of the primary object, often quite drastically. The process may be seen in the simple example: 'Gaius [primary object] is a toad [secondary object].' The analogy with chapters 2 and 4 suggests that one should look for some features of everyday human experience as constituting the primary objects of the various entities mentioned in the visionary sections of Daniel 7. There is no doubt that one primary object is Antiochus IV Epiphanes and that the images of the fourth beast and the horn constitute the secondary objects with which he is brought into conjunction. The preferable view of the primary object of the holy ones who are attacked by the beast but ultimately vindicated, a view taken by many British commentators (Barrett 1959; Moule 1982; Casey 1986), is that it consists of the Israelites who were persecuted by Antiochus and has no reference, for example, to the angels (as argued by Noth 1966, Collins 1977 and Reid 1989). Similarly, it is submitted that the figure described as 'one like a human being' in 7.13 is a corporate image for these Israelites and does not refer to a messiah, either angelic (so Collins 1977) or of

any other kind. Unfortunately, to substantiate these identifica-
tions requires a detailed argument which would extend beyond
the boundaries of this work.

Some further delineation of the nature and plight of the 'holy
ones' is possible. We are not expressly told if they comprise all of
Israel or only some particular group within Israel loyal to Yahweh, although the intimacy of the relationship suggested in the
phrase 'holy ones of the Most High' seems to imply the latter. Nor
does the vision reveal whether some of them had been killed,
although this too is surely implied in the notion that Antiochus
had prevailed against them (7.21). Finally, the focus is on the
attack on the Law, with the Temple not being mentioned here,
which may suggest that the person or circle responsible for the
work did not represent the priests. The relief offered to those
affected by the persecution is that sovereignty and power will be
transferred from Antiochus to the holy ones. This is a project for
the future, since the Seleucid king is still alive at the time of the
vision (7.26). Judged by this vision alone, the prospect envisaged
may be the establishment of a Jewish kingdom in Israel to replace
that of the Seleucids, although plainly some sort of heavenly
intervention is foreshadowed (7.26), which will lead to their
destruction. The vindication being held out is both political and
eschatological. Yet there is nothing in the text to suggest that the
holy ones should do anything to bring about this result, nor that a
leader will arise to lead such an enterprise, in the manner of the
millennial movements known to us from modern preindustrial
societies. Moreover, it is impossible to determine from Daniel 7
whether it was written for a millennial movement existing in the
wider Israelite population or merely expressed a millennial outlook held by a few within Israel. Unlike many modern millennial
movements, no messianic figure appears in Daniel 7.

Whatever the nature of the original audience of the work,
however, it plainly gives expression to a millennial outlook which
has come into existence by reason of the serious forms of deprivation being suffered by many Israelites. Underlying the imagery in
this vision are themes of the primordial subjugation of sea monsters going far back in Mesopotamian and Canaanite myth . But in
Daniel 7 these themes are given a very contemporary orientation
by means of the interpretation of the four beasts as a sequence of
four kingdoms and the elaboration of the one of them as illustra-
tive of a contemporary Seleucid king. Within the apocalyptic

framework, ancient imagery is utilised as the vehicle for articulating a response, in the form of a new myth, to the experience of political oppression in the present. The social function of this mythopoesis, as with the contemporary examples mentioned above, is to reassure the readers of the vision that another order of reality exists and that the terrible events of their present and recent past are occurring within a context controlled by heavenly forces who will ultimately restore the fortunes of the holy ones. This reassurance reaches its most exalted point in the identification in 7.18 of the holy ones of the Most High with 'one like a Son of Man' upon whom God confers power and honour and sovereignty (7.14), the most valuable of goods in this culture. By this device the holy ones, however persecuted they may be by Antiochus, have the knowledge of being participants in a heavenly drama in which they will eventually be vindicated.

Although this form of mythopoesis involves the creation of hope for a glorious future, that is hardly its only function. For a futurist myth like this one creates an experience in the present of the realities to which it refers and by evoking a vision of the deliverance in store for the chosen ones reinforces their social identity at a time when it is exposed to the greatest threat. The author of Daniel 7 seems to have had no precedent for such a use of myth, and the apocalyptic genre, to lay down a blueprint for the future of God's suffering ones in the face of grievous oppression. The vision in Daniel 7 represents a triumphantly novel application of the genre. In Daniel 7, therefore, in its vision of the fourth beast and its destruction which will inaugurate the transfer of power, honour and sovereignty to God's holy ones, we have an example of the prescriptive use of myth, to speak not of the past as the basis for the way things are, but of the future as the pattern of what they will become. As in the cargo cults of the South Pacific and the Ghost Dance of the American Indians, myth is employed in a radically novel way to tell of the coming transformation of the troubled present into a glorious future. Thus, even across oceans and millennia, indigenous peoples, caught in the iron jaws of the conquering beast, fashion for themselves similar myths of deliverance and exaltation.

Chapter 7

The social function of 4 Ezra

The Jewish apocalypse entitled 4 Ezra presents itself as a work composed by a Jewish exile in Babylon some thirty years after the destruction of Solomon's Temple by the Babylonians in 587 BCE. The actual apocalypse (leaving aside an introduction added later) begins like this:

> In the thirtieth year after the destruction of our city, I, Salathiel, who am also called Ezra, was in Babylon. I was troubled as I lay on my bed and my thoughts welled up in my heart, because I saw the desolation of Zion and the wealth of those who lived in Babylon. My spirit was greatly agitated and I began to speak anxious words to the Most High.
>
> (3.1–3; Stone 1990: 53)

The work actually dates to the end of the first century CE, but uses the dramatic garb of the earlier catastrophe to address issues thrown up by the devastation wreaked on Jerusalem and its population by the Romans in 70 CE. It is a work of towering moral integrity and imaginative power. According to Michael Stone in his recent commentary on 4 Ezra, however, little can be known of its 'social matrix and function'. He observes that we 'do not know how the book functioned and to whom it was directed' and is willing to venture the following as the only more or less secure facts known of 4 Ezra: first, that it was written in response to the destruction of the second Temple and expressed yearning for the end of the Roman Empire and the vindication of Israel; and secondly, that it seems to have been composed in Hebrew in Israel, about 100 CE (Stone 1990: 40 and 1987: 216). Professor Stone is hardly a lone voice in raising the problem of determining the social context and function of the apocalypses (Collins 1987: 29–30; Davies 1989: 251–71).

My aim in this chapter is to suggest, by use of various social-scientific perspectives, how 4 Ezra, our second 'fourth beast' text, may have functioned socially for its audience. In taking this course it is salutary to take seriously the warning of John J. Collins, that although sociological or anthropological models may well prove to be illuminating in studying the apocalypses, their valid use must presuppose an adequate literary understanding of the works in question (Collins 1987: 29). We should be wary, however, not to erect a false dichotomy, between social-scientific approaches and close literary readings of the text. Time and again the social sciences raise questions which can only be answered after careful literary examination.

SOCIAL-SCIENTIFIC PERSPECTIVES: COGNITIVE DISSONANCE AND INTROVERSIONISM

In the previous chapter I discussed two ways in which an introversionist movement might come into existence: first, as a reaction fuelled by the cognitive dissonance attending a failed millennial dream and, secondly, as an autonomous development among an indigenous people whose culture had been dislocated through contact with a technologically superior civilisation. The first type of introversionism can be illustrated by reference to the Ringatu church in New Zealand and the second by reference to the religion of an Iroquois Indian, Handsome Lake. I will now briefly describe these movements to establish the basis for a 'remote comparison' with 4 Ezra.

The Ringatu church

The Ringatu church, as described by Wilson (1975: 397–402), represents an instance of an introversionist religious movement which developed after the defeat of a revolutionist faith, in this case the Hau Hau movement among the Maoris in the 1860s. Following the defeat of the Maoris in warfare, which reflected a revolutionist response to white occupation, millennialism no longer seemed a viable option. The founder of the Ringatu faith, one Te Kooti Rikirangi, although he had not fought alongside the Hau Hau rebels, was deported with them to the Chatham Islands and imprisoned. While there he began to develop a new religion and in 1868 planned and executed a dramatic escape from the island with a large number of men, women and children. Initially he engaged in skirmishes with certain other Maoris and with the white authorities but he eventually settled down and from about 1873 onwards to his death in 1893 preached his religion. The Ringatu faith comprised a mixture of old Maori custom and biblical teaching. In particular, there was a stress on the literal application of the Old Testament stories to the Maoris as a people in bondage. Monthly meetings occurred, with a strong communal character, which was reinforced by the use of ancient Maori songs. The concerns of the Ringatu church were distinctively ethnic. They involved the withdrawal of a remnant who were members of an ethnic group to preserve a distinctive way of life. Its concept of salvation was less that of the elected saints of God than of a cultural community. It first arose among former members of the Hau Hau movement and plainly provided an alternative religious response which satisfied their needs once the prospect of millennial transformation had disappeared. A belief in some future transformation does not seem to have figured in Ringatu belief.

The religion of Handsome Lake

On other occasions, however, an introversionist movement will spring up autonomously among disturbed indigenous people who have not previously experienced millennial expectations and their disappointment. So it was with the religious movement among the Iroquois Indians founded by Handsome Lake at the end of the eighteenth century. The chief primary sources for this movement have been collected by Parker (1913) and Fenton (1968), while Wilson (1975: 387–97) and Wallace (1970: 239–337) offer excellent discussions of it. By the time of the American Revolutionary War, the Iroquois had experienced a long association with white settlers, which had led to the loss of land, diseases, widespread alcoholism, uprooted and lonely individuals and fragile social structures. During the war the Iroquois had sided with the British and the period after it was one of increased instability. The Quakers, a European introversionist sect, were interested in the Iroquois, not for proselytising, but to teach them how to cultivate the land and to spin, which the Quakers thought would lead the Indians into adopting desirable social and moral values. From 1798 to 1799 three Quakers lived among the Iroquois for this purpose. Although they did not seek to proselytise, they made plain their opposition to alcohol and other aspects of white culture and answered questions which the Indians raised about white religion. Many Indians, including one called Handsome Lake, who had been born in 1735, were impressed by the Quakers and their preoccupation with moral improvement.

At this time the practice of visiting the other world in dreams and returning with a message of repentance and reform was an established form of prophecy among the Iroquois . In June 1799 Handsome Lake began to have visions, some of which were written down by the Quakers then present and which were subsequently related to gatherings of the Iroquois (referred to as the Code of Handsome Lake). In his visions Handsome Lake beheld messengers who came to call him to repentance and who gave him an ethical teaching which he was to proclaim to the Iroquois. Alcohol was to be abandoned, witches condemned, family life was to be conducted along more disciplined and moral lines, theft, gossip, pride and cruelty to animals were proscribed, while repentance for sin, hospitality and mutual help were encouraged. Handsome Lake advocated a mixture of the best from Indian and Christian traditions. This new religion was called Gaiwiio, or 'The Good Word'.

Part of the message which Handsome Lake received consisted of predictions of the time of the End, when famine and plague would appear, wonders would occur, the earth would be destroyed by fire and the wicked would suffer damnation. Thus one part of the Code reads: 'Now it is said that you must relate what the messengers say about the coming end of the earth. Relate how all those who refuse to believe in Gaiwiio will suffer hardships' (Fenton 1968: 58). Those who had been virtuous on earth, however, would enjoy blessings thereafter. But the End which he predicted was not expected for three generations (Wallace 1970: 250; Wilson 1975: 393). Accordingly, although there was a millennial element to the teaching of Handsome Lake, the movement which he founded could in no way be described as revolutionist. His message concerning the End was more akin to the formal millennial teaching of orthodox Christian denominations than that of revolutionist sects, where it forms the very core of their response to the world. The modest millennial aspect of the

religion of Handsome Lake constituted an adjunct and an inducement to the ethical prescriptions which formed its heart. Bryan
Wilson has aptly described the Code as an attempt to restore the
dignity of the Iroquois life not through the old military virtues,
but through 'the acceptance of a separate way of life, and the quiet
fulfilment of ethical obligations' (1975: 396).

COGNITIVE DISSONANCE

Since considerable use will be made below of the notion of
cognitive dissonance, it is desirable to raise two issues with respect
to it. The first is a caveat as to the appropriateness of the notion at
all. The human drive to reduce dissonance, first explained in
detail by Leon Festinger (1957), should be seen not as a law
governing the behaviour of individuals or groups, for there are
no such laws, but rather as a useful model for certain phenomena.
As Bruce Malina has argued (1986), the existence of dissonance
presupposes a norm in a culture with respect to which inconsistency will produce doubt, distress or anxiety. Some social
situations, however, are riddled with inconsistency to such an
extent that dissonance becomes virtually normative. If so, Festinger's explanation of cognitive dissonance will be inappropriate,
even as a model. Nevertheless, it is clear that the author of 4 Ezra
and presumably his readers did consider that the sack of
Jerusalem in 70 CE and the enslavement and exile of many Jews
thereafter were grossly inconsistent with theological views on the
election of Israel and the significance of the Temple. In this
context there is room for the use of cognitive dissonance as a
model of human behaviour.

Secondly, as R.B. Abelson has argued (Abelson *et al.* 1968: 6),
responses to dissonance are best understood as rationalising
rather than necessarily rational modes of adaptation. Men and
women seek to cope with dissonance in ways which appear
rational to them and hopefully to others. But to outsiders who are
not convinced of the efficacy of the means being employed to
reduce dissonance, the whole enterprise will represent a
rationalisation of the problem.

MAORIS, IROQUOIS AND POST-70 CE JEWS – A BROAD COMPARISON

The broad comparability of these two religious movements and the situation of 70 CE Palestinian Jews is quickly shown. Like the Maoris who eventually became members of the Ringatu movement, the Jews had been defeated by a colonising power in a confrontation which had certain millennial undertones. A revolutionist response to political oppression constituted the background of both. In each case defeat had brought economic deprivation and even deportation of some of the local people. Like the Iroquois, the Jews had lost much of their traditional land. For the Jews, however, the devastation was on a far greater scale, as expressed by Ezra as follows:

> For you see that
> our sanctuary has been laid waste,
> our altar thrown down,
> our temple destroyed;
> our harp has been laid low,
> our song has been silenced,
> and our rejoicing has been ended;
> the light of our lampstand has been put out,
> the ark of our covenant has been plundered,
> our holy things have been polluted,
> and the name by which we are
> called has been profaned;
> our free men have suffered abuse,
> our priests have been burned to death,
> our Levites have gone into captivity;
> our virgins have been defiled,
> and our wives have been ravished;
> our righteous men have been carried off,
> our little ones have been cast out,
> our young men have been enslaved,
> and our strong men made powerless.
>
> (10.21–22; Stone 1990: 316–17)

The theological problem arising from this is posed at the very start of the work when Ezra asks why Babylon, whose sins are without number, has gained dominion over Zion (3.27–31). Shortly after, the economic consequences are laid bare when Ezra complains that Israel and Jacob have not received the reward of their labours, while the other nations which do not keep the commandments abound in wealth (3.33). Perhaps the most striking feature of the comparison is in the fact that in the sixth part of the work, the vision of the man from the sea, it is revealed that among the multitude which the Messiah gathers to himself are the nine and a half tribes led away by the Assyrians in the time of King Hoshea, of whom it is stated:

> But they formed this plan for themselves, that they would leave the multitude of the nations and go to a more distant region, where no human race had ever lived, that there at least they might keep their statutes which they had not kept in their own land. And they went in by the narrow passages of the Euphrates river. For at that time the Most High performed wonders for them, and stopped the springs of the river until they had passed over. To that region there was a long way to go, a journey of a year and a half; and that country is called Arzareth.
>
> (13.41–5; Stone 1990: 393)

Although this might reflect a purely legendary tradition (Stone 1990: 404), rather than originating in any experience of actual withdrawal, it is noteworthy that such an introversionist outlook, so consonant with the geographic segregation adopted by defeated indigenous peoples in recent times, should feature in the text.

The position of the Palestinian Jews who survived the revolt, whether in Palestine or deported abroad, including the author and audience of 4 Ezra, may therefore be compared to that of modern preindustrial peoples who reacted to colonisation with millennial expectations and armed revolt, only to experience the failure of both in a catastrophe which shattered or grossly disturbed their culture and religion. The extent of the deprivation suffered by Israel is eloquently expressed in 10.21–2. For these Jews, as with some modern indigenous peoples so afflicted, the aftermath of the events of 66–73 CE also brought with it strong cognitive dissonance. The intense discrepancy between the hopes which had been focused on Jerusalem and the reality of its destruction provides the dynamic underlying the development in the work. As already noted, if the conditions are right, cognitive dissonance gives rise to pressures to reduce it and such pressures are very obviously present in 4 Ezra. The central achievement of the work consists in the reduction (if not complete elimination) of the dissonance present at the start. From a theological perspective, 4 Ezra represents an exercise in theodicy (see Thompson 1977).

The comparison reveals one feature in 4 Ezra, however, which is without parallel among the Ringatu or Handsome Lake religions, namely, that the text transcends preoccupation with the fate of the Jews as a result of the events of 67–73 CE. Even though the fact that Israel had been devastated by the Romans constitutes the *raison d'être* of the work, the text expresses a genuine concern for non-Israelites. For this reason 4 Ezra is a work of striking moral amplitude.

THE LITERARY STRUCTURE OF 4 EZRA

The work comprises seven distinct episodes. The first three (3.1– 5.20a, 5.20b–6.34 and 6.35–9.25) are dialogues between Ezra and Uriel. Their subject is largely a sceptical questioning by Ezra, reminiscent of Job, as to how the justice of God might be reconciled with the destruction of Zion and the fact that so few human beings will be saved, together with replies by Uriel. The fourth episode (9.26–10.59) consists of the description of a woman, mourning for the loss of her son, who is dramatically transformed into a city (10.25–7), coupled with Uriel's explanation of the meaning of these events. After this vision and its interpretation, there are three further visions in which the scepticism which characterises the earlier parts of 4 Ezra largely disappears; indeed, the views proposed by the angel in the dialogues in the first three episodes, which Ezra opposes, are largely adopted by him in his farewell speech in 14.28–36 (Stone 1990: 16, commenting on the views of Harnisch and Brandenburger).

Most commentators agree that the critical issue for the interpretation of the work is how to account for inconsistencies which are alleged to beset it, especially the difficulty of reconciling the first three dialogues with the rest. Although widely divergent approaches are taken on this issue, nearly all of them propose some view of the author's personality to explain the transformation of the seer from sceptic into believer. Broadly speaking, critics tend to favour one or other of two lines of interpretation: either to see Ezra as representing the author's own doubts which are only resolved with difficulty (H. Gunkel, W. Harrelson and

A.L. Thompson), or to regard Uriel as representative of the author's views, while Ezra stands for a position the author condemns (E. Brandenburger and W. Harnisch). These are all heavily dependent on views as to the author's personality.

Michael E. Stone has recently advanced an account of the structure of the work which offers an intriguing explanation for the alleged anomaly of Ezra's transformation. Stone suggests that the angel 'represents that part of himself which wishes to accept but is forced to doubt by the impact of events' (1990: 32) and that in the first three sections Ezra and the angel are Janus faces of the author's self. When Ezra meets the woman mourning over her son in the fourth section he encounters his own pain and distress externalised. He seeks first to rebuke and then to console her by reminding her of the far greater tragedy of the destruction of Jerusalem (10.21–2). In comforting her Ezra undergoes a dramatic change, a conversion. During her address (9.43–10.4) the woman expresses an outlook he himself exhibited in the first three sections. In a striking reversal of roles, Ezra now takes on the attitude to her which the angel previously expressed to him.

These views that the meaning of the work can only be addressed by reference to some putative attitudes of the author suffer from two fundamental *prima facie* difficulties. First of all, they fail to take into account the tensions inevitably attending dissonance and its reduction, in particular the fact that the process often seems to outsiders to involve an unconvincing rationalisation. Secondly, they ignore the problem of tying explanations of the meaning of a text to an authorial personality which is utterly unknown. Added to this a literary examination of the text itself casts doubt upon such modes of analysis and, in the light of the social-scientific perspectives outlined above, suggests a quite different explanation.

Analysis of the vision of the mourning woman

Apart from a number of textual features pointing to a change in the focus of the work prior to the appearance of the bereaved woman (8.55, 9.13, 9.24–5 and 9.37), the actual way Ezra's encounter with the woman is structured runs counter to Stone's view that it is the process of consolation which produces the transformation. As soon as he sees the woman, with rent clothes and ashes on her head, Ezra dismisses his previous reflections (9.39–40). In so doing he complies with Uriel's earlier direction to him – 'Do not continue to be curious as to how the ungodly will be punished' (9.13). Shortly after he reiterates that he has broken off his earlier reflections (10.5) and then proceeds to address her, first in rebuke and then in consolation. Thus, the focus of the work shifts in a fundamental way *before* he has begun to console her. In Ezra's address to the woman he reminds her of the magnitude of the disaster which has fallen upon Zion, compared with which her grief is insignificant, and holds out to her the prospect of personal consolation. He counsels her to trust in God's justice and mercy.

Yet it is not what Ezra says to the woman which irrevocably terminates the anguished doubts of the dialogues and replaces them with the triumphant visions of the future in the second half of the work. This momentous change is effected by the astounding vision of the woman transformed into a city resting on huge foundations (10.25–8) and the angel's interpretation of this event (10.29–59). The vision is Ezra's first visual experience of a supernatural kind in the work. Hitherto his discussions with the angel were conducted in a rational and low-key manner. In each of the three dialogues he prefaces the angel's address with a brief statement to the effect that the angel was sent to him (4.1, 5.31 and 7.1), but there is no numinous aspect whatever to the angel's arrival. In this respect, the description of the angel in the dialogues in 4 Ezra is reminiscent of the similarly understated angelophany in Zechariah 1.9.

The orderly, if passionate, discussion concerning God's justice, begun between Ezra and the angel and continued in his advice to the woman, is dramatically overshadowed by her awesome metamorphosis, which induces in him a terror and bewilderment he has not previously expressed. It is made clear in the text, moreover, that the new reaches of human experience into which Ezra is transported by this vision involve a privation of his rational faculties. He describes his condition upon the arrival of Uriel in answer to his call (10.28) as follows: 'I lay there like a corpse and I was deprived of my understanding' (10.30; Stone 1990: 329). A little later he says:

> I did as you directed, and, behold, I saw, and still see, what I am unable to explain . . . For I have seen what I did not know, and I have heard what I do not understand. Or is my mind deceived, and my soul dreaming?
>
> (10.32–36: Stone 1990: 329)

At this point he seeks an explanation from Uriel of what has happened (10.37). His comment that he has seen what he did not know, although intended to refer to the mystery of the woman's transformation, aptly describes the movement in the work from the dialogues of the first half to the visions of the second. Truth which was difficult for Ezra to accept in the to-and-fro of rational debate becomes accessible when the mode of instruction shifts from the cognitive to the visionary.

This conclusion is supported by an analysis of the angel's interpretation of the vision (10.38–59). Here there is presented a direct equivalence between Ezra's situation in the dialogues and that in his dealings with the woman. In each instance he is mourning over Zion, at first during the course of rational discussion and then dramatically and symbolically in his treatment of the woman. In other words, Ezra's dealings with her represent exactly the same process of mourning, but at a symbolic and visionary level. Nothing new happens in this section of the work; it contains rather a reworking of the earlier material at a different level of human experience.

The use of the vision of the woman who becomes a city is a bold and strikingly successful literary device. To account for its success, assistance may be obtained from a key notion of the literary theory of the Russian formalists – the notion of defamiliarisation. According to Shklovsky, literary language (which is plainly present in 4 Ezra even though it is not a purely literary work) defamiliarises habituated ideas and sensations and allows us to 'recover the sensation of life'. For art 'exists to make one feel things, to make the stone *stony*. The purpose of art is to impart the sensation of things as they are perceived and not as they are known.' A literary image 'creates a vision of the object instead of serving as a means of knowing it' (Rice and Waugh 1990: 17–21, a convenient extract of Shklovsky's views). What Ezra experienced in his vision of the woman (just as did the original audience of the work) is precisely this process of defamiliarisation. The sorrow of Israel he had always known; the destiny of Israel he had anxiously discussed. Yet when he actually sees sorrowing Israel and then the glories of her future he does not recognise her and falls into a state of deep shock. The defamiliarization of what he has always known, the replacement of knowledge with vision, is beyond his powers of assimilation. He requires the angel Uriel to explain it to him.

EZRA AS REPRESENTATIVE OF ISRAEL

In coming to this realisation, Ezra should be seen as representative of Israel. E. Breech reached a similar view in an important article in 1973 in which he proposed that Ezra was a prophet and that in articulating his difficulties with divine justice and in progressing from sorrow to consolation he represented the wider Jewish community (1973). Breech noted that the community has been entrusted to Ezra, like a flock to its shepherd (5.17–18); he is, in fact, its last prophet (12.42). He prays on their behalf (12.48; 1973: 271). Moreover, most important (although not mentioned in this context by Breech) are the two considerations that Ezra shares the fate of Israel – 'for Zion, the mother of us all, is in deep grief and great affliction' (10.7) – and that he is the agent through whom the people once again receive the Law (14.45).

The Jewish revolt of 67–63 CE and its aftermath represented a shattering blow to the very pillars supporting Jewish ethnic identity. These events had a profound social, political, economic and even psychological significance which must be taken into account when seeking to understand the context from within which and to which 4 Ezra was written. It is the total impact of the Roman victory and the intense cognitive dissonance this caused by reason of the Jews' belief in their election by God which must be considered. In charting the course by which the prophet Ezra reaches a resolution of these difficulties, the text offers to all Jews so troubled a mode of reconciling themselves to the issues thrown up by the tragedy of the revolt. In particular, the visions which are revealed to Ezra become the property of all who read the work. They provide to readers of 4 Ezra a mode of access to the glories which are to come.

The dissonance affected a whole people and was plainly not of the type which could easily be tolerated, let alone become normative. Such dissonance often produces an effort to reduce it, and where it is of this magnitude the need for it to be modified may well be quite urgent (Carroll 1979: 91). At its most fundamental level, the social function of 4 Ezra is to provide a mode of reducing the almost unbearable dissonance which beset the Jewish people after 70 CE to an acceptable level. In that task, the vision of the mourning woman plays a central part. Particular strategies, introversionist in nature and involving eschatology and the Law, adopted to achieve this result will now be considered.

ESCHATOLOGY

4 Ezra contains a clearly delineated eschatological calendar. First come 'signs', messianic woes, which are described in several places in the text (5.1–13, 6.20–4 and 9.1–4). Then the Redeemer figure/ Messiah will appear (7.28–9). The next stage commences with the death of the Messiah and all those with him, which presages the return of the world to its primordial silence for seven days, a common mythical motif analysed by Mircea Eliade (1989). Lastly comes the judgement with the good souls going to heaven and the bad to hell (7.30–44).

The precise way in which the role of the Messiah is described is very significant. In the first section the angel tells Ezra:

> For my Messiah shall be revealed with those who are with him, and he shall make rejoice those who remain for four hundred years, and after these years my son [or: servant] the Messiah shall die, and all who draw human breath.
>
> (7.28–9; Stone 1990: 202)

In the eagle vision (11.18–12.51) the role of the Messiah is more precisely specified. As mentioned in the previous chapter of this book, he will first rebuke and then destroy the eagle, which is explicitly identified with the fourth beast (12.11), a metaphor which has as its primary object the Roman Empire, and then tend to his people as follows: 'He will deliver in mercy the remnant of my people, those who have been saved throughout my borders, and he will make them joyful until the end comes, the day of judgment' (12.34; Stone 1990: 360). Lastly, the angel's interpretation of the vision of the man from the sea contains a general statement of his role, including the fact that 'he will direct those who are left' (13.26). This precedes a more general description of how he will achieve this which concludes with the following verses: 'And it will be when he destroys the multitude of the nations that are gathered together, he will defend the people who remain. And then he will show them very many wonders' (13.49–50; Stone 1990: 394).

It is of fundamental importance that in these images of the events which will precede the Last Judgement, especially the 400 year messianic period, there is no suggestion that the people themselves will play any active role, for example, by taking part in the hostilities. They are merely to enjoy the consequences of the Messiah's action. Nor, indeed, is there any suggestion, as there is

in the vision in Daniel 7.27, that they will receive political authority or the honour or prestige attaching to it. Finally, the role of the
Messiah is a non-political one. He is not described as a king, nor is
the period of his dispensation referred to as a kingdom (Stone
1987: 217). These considerations seem to be related to the situation at the time 4 Ezra was composed. With Israel still devastated
by the Roman conquest some thirty years or so earlier, the work
does not advocate or even refer to the type of vindication which
would involve participation by Jews in destroying Rome. To this
extent their situation parallels that of other indigenous peoples,
such as the Maoris of New Zealand, for whom decisive military
defeat spelled the end of active resistance to colonial occupation
and even millennial dreams of their enemies' political authority
reverting to its rightful possessors.

It might be thought, however, that the mere fact that the text
foretells the demise of the Roman Empire and of evil nations
generally indicates that a strong emphasis falls upon holding out
to the Israelites the prospect of vindication against their enemies
in the political arena. Yet militating against this view is the fact, as
just seen, that they will play no part in destroying the eagle and
that the Messiah will not inaugurate a kingdom of a political kind.

More significant than this, however, is the fact that the foreshadowed End is not imminent, in spite of the views of Michael
Stone to the contrary (Stone 1990: 417). In dealing with this
subject it seems essential to heed the warnings of Bruce Malina to
take into account the very different attitude to time held by first-
century inhabitants of the Mediterranean region as compared
with that current today (Malina 1989). It is impossible within the
bounds of this chapter, however, adequately to canvass this issue.
Nevertheless, there is considerable evidence against the notion
that the text envisages an imminent End. Although in the first
segment of the work Ezra is told that the world 'is hastening
swiftly to its end' (4.26), it soon becomes clear that there is a
considerable time to elapse before this will occur. In the same
section of the work and shortly after this Ezra asks whether more
time is to come (that is, until the End) than has passed, or whether
the greater part has gone by (4.45). He is told that the situation is
like a rainstorm, which has poured down heavy rain leaving drops
remaining in the cloud; in other words, that the proportion that
has passed is far greater (4.50), but not that the End is imminent.
In the next section the angel compares the situation with that of a

'creation which already is ageing and passing the strength of youth' (5.55). Once again, however, this image allows for a considerable period still to elapse; it is not suggested that the death of creation is imminent. The statement of the angel in the third section that 'my judgement is now drawing near' (8.61) is equally inexplicit. In the eagle vision it is said that the destruction of the eagle will occur at 'the end of the times' (12.9), but not when this will occur. It is a mistaken approach, moreover, to attempt to interpret the particular details of the eagle vision as relating to this or that aspect of the history of Roman domination. Such a one-dimensional reading of the text wrongly assumes that apocalyptic symbols are 'mere codes whose meaning is exhausted by single referents' (Collins 1987: 13). The correct position is that at this point in the text the author, like the writers of other apocalypses, is vaguely alluding to aspects of Roman rule as material for prophetic creation, rather than setting out the future cryptographically.

That the End is not imminent is also confirmed in the last section of the work. Here God tells Ezra:

> For the age has lost its youth, and the times begin to grow old. For the age is divided into twelve parts, and nine of its parts have already passed, as well as half of the tenth part, so two of its parts remain, besides half of the tenth part.
>
> (14.10–12; Stone 1990: 414)

At the end of this section we learn that this vision has occurred 5000 years after creation (14.49). If one were to assume that the twelve parts referred to in 14.11 are of equal duration, since nine and one-half twelfths of the total period of time equal 5000 years, simple arithmetic suggests that the total period envisaged is some 6315 years or that creation will endure for some 1315 years beyond the death of Ezra. Given the dramatic date for the death of Ezra is about 555 BCE, people reading the text in 100 CE might assume that it is suggesting that there are some 660 years to go before the End. While it may be the case that the original readers of the text would not have carried out such computations, it is apparent that even a cursory comparison of the time-scale in the last vision with its dramatic date would not leave an original reader with any expectation that the end was imminent. In this respect the eschatological calendar parallels that in the visions of Handsome Lake in which, it will be recalled, there was an End foreshadowed, but not for three generations. The prospect of a period of existence in this world which 4 Ezra offers to its readers is related to the emphasis in the work on continued adherence to the Mosaic Law. This aspect must now be explored.

THE CONTINUING ROLE OF THE LAW

The principal issue concerning the Law thrown up by the comparative material mentioned earlier is whether it is presented as a mode of maintaining a separate Jewish identity during the period leading up to the End in a manner similar to the ethnic isolation of the Ringatu faith or the fulfilment of ethical obligations among the Iroquois. This way of approaching the problem has the advantage of being rooted in the comparable experience of other indigenous peoples and allows us, in seeking to determine the meaning of the text for its original audience, to recognise and hopefully guard against the tendency to interpret it in the light of presuppositions, often unstated, originating in twentieth-century outlooks and concerns. The disadvantages of not taking this line can be seen in the view of E.P. Sanders that 'the problem posed by the book' is whether it provides an example of the collapse of 'covenantal nomism' and its replacement with 'legalistic perfectionism'; in other words, whether it reveals how Judaism works 'when it actually does become a religion of individual self-righteousness' (Sanders 1977: 409).

The bulk of the material on the Law in 4 Ezra is located in the first four sections. At an early stage (4.23) we learn that the discussion is taking place in a situation where the written record of the Law no longer exists. As we are informed later that the Law has been burned (14.21), it is clear that the reader is meant to understand that all copies of the Torah were destroyed in the onslaught of the 'Babylonians'. This feature is of considerable significance, given that the work ends with Ezra's dictating, under divine inspiration, twenty-four books, which are no doubt meant to be the corpus of Jewish scripture, and certain other works. The dramatic date for this event is about 557 BCE. In other words, one aim of the work is to proffer an aetiology of the Law's existence in spite of the catastrophe of 587 BCE. For the readers of 4 Ezra still suffering the trauma of the Roman victory in 67–73 CE, the insertion into the text of a claim that the Law had been given to

Israel on two separate occasions in the past could only serve to underline its continuing significance.

The most striking feature of the treatment of the Law in 4 Ezra is the extent to which it is related to eschatology. Time and again one encounters passages which affirm that salvation in the next world is dependent upon compliance with the Law in this one. A notable instance occurs in the description of the Last Judgement in 7.32–44, in particular in the following passage:

> Then the pit of torment shall appear,
> and opposite it shall be the place of rest;
> and the furnace of Gehenna shall be disclosed,
> and opposite it the paradise of delight.
>
> Then the Most High will say to the
> nations that have been raised,
> 'Look and understand
> whom you have denied,
> whom you have not served,
> whose commandments you have despised!
> Look opposite you:
> here are delight and rest,
> and there are fire and torments!'
>
> (7.36–38; Stone 1990: 203)

A similar theme is presented at 7.70–4 and at 7.79–101. It is not easy to envisage a more determined attempt than this to relate the necessity of compliance with the Law to the eschatological teaching of the Last Judgement. This emphasis brings to mind the function of the millennial dimension in reinforcing ethics in the teaching of Handsome Lake. To further tease out the implications of this comparison, however, we must consider the role of the Law in the period preceding the End, which we have argued above forms an essential part of the eschatological calendar of 4 Ezra, especially as it is presented in the last section of the work (chapter 14).

From the description in chapter 14 of how God came to transmit the Law to Israel through Ezra (with Ezra being virtually presented as a second Moses), it emerges that the function of the Law in the work is to provide to Israel, to Ezra's people, the guidance they will need in the time prior to the end of the world. Israel is offered, in effect, a second chance to observe the Law, in spite of its earlier transgressions. The corporate dimension of this message is very strong. The ultimate message in the text as far as the Law is concerned is not directed to individuals, nor to a group within Israel, sectarian (as argued by Overman 1990) or otherwise, but to Israel as a whole. The visions of the future, especially of the Last Judgement, are closely linked to the role of the Law. Compliance with its requirements in the present will result in mercy in the next world, while failure to comply will lead to eternal damnation. The emphasis in all this is far removed from the religion of legalistic perfectionism and individual self-righteousness which E.P. Sanders has claimed to have discovered in the text. Individualism, which in any event is a concept more at home in modern consciousness than in the very different social system of the first-century Mediterranean world (Malina 1981: 51–70), is not a primary interest in 4 Ezra, since its focus is the fate of Israel.

Compliance with the Law has a similar function in 4 Ezra to the ethnic isolation of the Ringatu movement and the fulfilment of ethical obligations in the religion of Handsome Lake. The Law provides a mode of behaviour which will ensure the continued existence of a Jewish people and a Jewish identity at a time when the Temple, the other institution once central to that identity, lies in ruins. The hope of eschatological reward and the prospect of eternal damnation are proposed as motivations, respectively, of the carrot and stick variety, for keeping the Law. Yet it is keeping the Law which matters. Although the text invokes a rich panoply of apocalyptic features to bring before its readers divine revelation of a future alternatively blessed or terrible, these are matters for the future, possibly a quite distant one. Compliance with the Law, however, starts here and now.

Apocalyptic vision may no doubt serve as an effective carrier for various messages but here the message is the Law. Once that message is accepted, moreover, it is likely that the necessity for continuing revelation would become attenuated, as the existence and identity of the Jewish people became increasingly predicated upon adherence to the numerous requirements of the Law. In the result, although it is the apocalyptic genre which is employed in 4 Ezra to mediate the Law to the Jewish people across the tragedy of Roman conquest, in the end, by so doing, it would seem to have the potential to hasten its own demise. Accordingly, it is no surprise that in the second or third centuries CE, although the composition of a Jewish legal corpus proceeded apace, there are signs (disputed in some quarters) that interest in apocalyptic literature waned. Thus, although certain aspects of the Jewish apocalyptic tradition survived – for example, messianic expectation (Collins 1987: 206) and *merkavah* mysticism (which deals with visionary ascents to heaven) (Rowland 1985: 272) – works like 4 Ezra do not seem to have been written after about 100 CE, and survived among Christians and not Jews. Moreover, as Michael Stone has suggested, 4 Ezra shows clear connections with rabbinic circles, especially in certain exegetical and theological areas, even if it is not itself a rabbinic work (Stone 1990: 38–9). These considerations suggest that 4 Ezra stands in a pivotal position between the types of Judaism which existed prior to the events of 70 CE and that which would come into existence under the pervasive influence of the Mishnah.

CONCLUSION: THE SOCIAL FUNCTION OF 4 EZRA

The situation of the original Jewish audience for whom 4 Ezra was written, victims of the fourth beast, provides the key to understanding its social function. They had been shattered by military conquest, denuded of their wealth and led off, many of them, into captivity in foreign lands, while the Temple, their central ethnic and religious institution, had been destroyed. Unlike many other indigenous peoples who had suffered a similar fate, however, the Jews had a highly developed theological tradition which stressed that they were God's chosen people among all the races of the earth. In the face of their total defeat by Rome this doctrine of election produced a powerful dissonance, an agonising discrepancy between what their religious beliefs suggested should happen and their actual experience. The primary social function of 4 Ezra was to provide a means of managing or eliminating this dissonance. It communicated to its original readers a resolution of this tension and a basis for Israel's continued existence embodied in literary form. By charting the course by which Ezra, Israel's prophet and representative, eventually came to reconcile the grim events of recent history and larger problems of evil with a theological tradition asserting God's favour and mercy, the text offered the same resolution to its first audience. Ezra's journey from grief to hope was, vicariously, Israel's. In particular, the movement from a rational to a visionary mode of cognition dramatically experienced by the seer in the transformation of the woman into Zion in the fourth episode operates as a highly successful example of defamiliarisation which the readers of the work could appropriate and benefit from at an imaginative and symbolical level.

Modern readers may find the progression from rational discourse where doubt reigns to vision where hope is triumphant an unconvincing rationalisation. But we are outsiders to the dissonance and the means used to reduce and eliminate it. There is no reason to suppose that the solution proffered in 4 Ezra was anything other than effective, especially in view of the powerful social pressures on communities whose existence is threatened by discordant cognitions to generate ways of eliminating them.

Yet 4 Ezra did not just speak to the distress of the present. It reached beyond that to the future and proposed a means by which Israel might survive. Here the comparability of its message with that of other introversionist movements is very evident. Although the text looks forward to a future and eternal redemption, that redemption is not imminent. The manner in which the work re-endorses the Law as the source of life for Israel (even to the extent of using eschatology as a way of securing compliance with its requirements) reveals how salvation has become a present endeavour. The text encourages Israel to gather around the Law in quiet fulfilment of its obligations. Subsequent centuries would reveal how this process, once begun, eventually became the preeminent expression of Jewish identity.

In the first three episodes of the work the concern expressed for humanity beyond Israel represents, in the context of Rome's treatment of the Jews, a triumph of Jewish ethical reflection. Yet the fact that at the end the focus has narrowed to the destiny of Israel alone indicates that the community itself is the source and seat of all salvation. Although it is not difficult to cite examples of other movements which by virtue of geographic or social isolation have been more introversionist than the Israel of 4 Ezra, the introversionist tendencies in the work are manifest.

Perhaps, then, we can afford to be a little more sanguine as to our prospects of discovering the social function of this particular apocalypse than has hitherto been recognised. The findings which have come from this investigation, moreover, have resulted from posing to the text questions originating in accessible and well-known social-scientific literature. We should hardly be surprised, however, if in seeking to investigate the social function of 4

Ezra our task is assisted more by avenues of intellectual enquiry specifically aimed at penetrating the social dimensions of human experience than by a criticism which refuses to avail itself of such assistance.

Chapter 8

Sorcery accusations and the Apocalypse

POLITICAL OPPRESSION IN THE APOCALYPSE?

The imagery of the beast in the Apocalypse, especially in chapter 13 with its allusions to the fourth beast and suffering holy ones of Daniel 7, raises the possibility that John and his readers were also caught up in the brutalities of imperial domination. As we have just seen, 4 Ezra, probably written about the same time as the Apocalypse, expressly links the Danielic fourth beast to the eagle, a creature which refers to Rome, whose eagle-bearing legions had devastated Jerusalem and killed, enslaved or exiled most of its population. Although one cannot demonstrate a direct connection between the Apocalypse and 4 Ezra, it would hardly be surprising if the author of the Christian work, who was heir to the same Jewish scriptural tradition, also turned to Daniel in a situation of Roman oppression. This is not to say, however, that John would have been interested in the same acts of domination, in particular the destruction of Jerusalem. Although the Apocalypse was probably written after 70 CE and in two passages at least seems to presuppose that the Temple has been destroyed (11.1–2 and 21.22), the fact of its destruction is of no great concern to the author, nor would one necessarily expect such concern from a Christian writer towards the end of the first century. Nevertheless, there is evidence that the beast is capable of at least one type of violence which was of great significance to the author – the martyrdom of Christians. Was the Apocalypse composed in response to actual or threatened persecution by Rome? Does such a context underlie the existence of the work or features of it?

There is little doubt that the work was written subsequent to a time in which a large number of Christians had been martyred. The general statement in 13.7 that the beast was allowed to make war on the saints and conquer them is corroborated by several other details in the text. Thus John sees the harlot of Babylon, an image which also refers to Rome, as 'drunk with the blood of the saints and the blood of the martyrs of Jesus' (17.6) and in the next chapter he confirms that 'in her was found the blood of prophets and of saints, and of all who have been slain on earth' (18.24). Rome is also to be seen as responsible for the deaths of those beheaded for their testimony to Jesus who are mentioned in 20.4. Most specific, however, is the reference to the 'huge crowd' (*ochlos polus* - 7.9) standing in front of God's throne who came through the great tribulation and washed their clothes in the blood of the Lamb (7.14). Behind these details may well be the Christians who were martyred by Nero in 64 CE. Terrible details of these events are given by Tacitus in the *Annals* (15.44), where he relates that a huge number (*multitudo ingens*) were condemned and then killed. This description is consonant with the 'huge number' of Apoc. 7.9 and the 'great persecution' of 7.14. The events of 64 CE must have sent shockwaves throughout the Christian communities, the re-verberations of which can still be felt in the Apocalypse, even though it was written some years later.

Yet the bleak depiction of Rome in the Apocalypse covers far more than its capacity for blood-letting. The text also makes much of the fact that the whole world was involved in worshipping this beast, together with Satan (13.11–18). This data clearly raises the issue of the imperial cult. The other beast, this time from the land, mentioned in 13.11, which wields the authority of the first beast and makes the inhabitants of the earth worship it, is probably an allusion to some person or institution whose role is to enforce the power and authority of Rome, perhaps in the local area. Simon Price has recently shown how prevalent and popular this cult was in Asia Minor in the first century (1984). Accordingly, although the meaning of the beast and its evil is not exhausted by the reference to Rome, it is difficult to escape the conclusion that this is part of the message being communicated by the text.

To appreciate the full extent to which Rome is presented as implicated in unjust domination, one must attend to the broader context of chapter 13, namely, the cycle of material running from 12.1 to 20.10 which deals with the appearance of the dragon, identified as, *inter alia*, Satan at 12.9, its activities, either on its own or through its agents such as the beasts of chapter 13, and its final defeat at 20.10. Much of the literary background to the combat

narrative which characterises this section of the Apocalypse has
been explored by A.Y. Collins (1976). The principal body of
existing literature and myth utilised in chapters 12–20 is that
dealing with Satan and the Watchers or fallen angels (see Forsyth
1987). A noteworthy feature of John's use of this material is the
extent to which he subverts or ironises his readers' expectations.
This becomes apparent as early as chapter 12. In 12.7–9 he
invokes the myth of the fall of Satan and his angels from heaven:

> Now war arose in heaven, Michael and his angels fighting
> against the dragon; and the dragon and his angels fought, but
> they were defeated and there was no longer any place for them
> in heaven. And the great dragon was thrown down, that
> ancient serpent, who is called the Devil and Satan, the deceiver
> of the whole world – he was thrown down to earth; and his
> angels were thrown down with him.

In Jewish circles of the first century this event was thought to have
occurred long before. Nevertheless, in the following verses a
remarkable reworking of this myth occurs:

> And I heard a loud voice in heaven, saying, 'Now the salvation
> and the power and the kingdom of our God and the authority
> of his Christ have come, for the accuser of our brethren has
> been thrown down, who accuses them day and night before our
> God. And they have conquered him by the blood of the Lamb
> and by the word of their testimony, for they loved not their lives
> even unto death.'

$$(12.10–11)$$

The characterisation of Satan as someone who accuses 'our
brethren' means that he is being presented as having a role with
respect to the followers of Jesus which he actually possessed long
before, at the time of his fall (cf. Job 2). Furthermore, by stating
that 'they' – which refers back to 'our brethren' – conquered him
(meaning Satan) through the blood of the Lamb and the proclamation of their witness, the text in these verses attributes the
fall of Satan to the activities of Christians in the present or the very
recent past, and not to the victory by Michael and his angels in
primordial times. Accordingly, in the cycle of stories which occupies 12.1–20.10 a vast myth is created which involves Satan and
Babylon (the primary object of which metaphor is Rome), on the
one hand, and the forces of good, both heavenly and terrestrial,

in the form of the followers of Jesus, on the other. This representation of the myth of Satan and the Watchers, with the Christians playing a key role, constitutes a bold venture into mythopoesis and one which indicates the author's propensity to exaggerate the role and plight of Christians in the larger cosmic order.

The extent to which Rome is denigrated, even demonised, in the Apocalypse prompts the insistent question of whether this work, just like Daniel 7 and 4 Ezra, employs the apocalyptic genre in a context of actual political oppression and has a social function of assisting the Christians for whom it was written to come to terms with such oppression in ways comparable with either the revolutionist or the introversionist response. Is the text, for example, engaging in millennial mythopoesis in a manner comparable to its use in the cargo cults of the South Pacific and the Ghost Dance of the American Indians, as a direct and unambiguous response to a current or impending attack by Rome on the early Christian movement among seven cities of Asia Minor? Or, alternatively, is the perspective of the Apocalypse more akin to the introversionism evident in the Ringatu religion of New Zealand or the movement founded by Handsome Lake? Although the preponderance of eschatology over ethics in the Apocalypse suggests that millennialism offers more promising comparative material, it is not possible within the ambit of this book to pursue such questions here. Nevertheless, whatever course one takes on this issue, the existence of threatened or actual political oppression by Rome is a matter of fundamental importance in the interpretation of the work. If there was no such oppression, how does one account for John's anti-Roman myth, which goes further in its extent and intensity than anything found in Daniel 7 or 4 Ezra?

Many commentators have located the Apocalypse in the context of actual persecution. John Gager, for example, has argued that the work was written to provide consolation at a time of suffering and death at the hands of Rome (1975: 50). According to Elizabeth Schüssler Fiorenza, the Christians for whom the work was written, probably, she says, during the reign of the increasingly totalitarian Domitian, were encountering harassment, persecution and hostility, especially by reason of their opposition to the Roman imperial cult (1985: 194). Views such as these which advocate, in effect, a political crisis for the Christians of Asia Minor have the virtue of taking seriously the animosity towards Rome and the delight which attends the prospect of Rome's demise (19.1–3):

> After this I heard what seemed to be the loud voice of a great multitude in heaven, crying, 'Hallelujah! Salvation and glory and power belong to our God, for his judgements are true and just; he has judged the great harlot who corrupted the earth with her fornication, and he has avenged on her the blood of his servants.' Once more they cried, 'Hallelujah! The smoke from her goes up for ever and ever.'

J.A.T. Robinson expressed this view very succinctly when he wrote that if there was no such crisis, Revelation would be the product of a perfervid and psychotic imagination (1976: 231).

One problem with this view is that it is not supported by what we know of the history of the period. The common notion that the reign of Domitian was a time of persecution of Christians has recently been the subject of critical reassessment. L. Thompson, for example, has argued that Domitian has been portrayed too negatively in much scholarly literature and that Christian urban dwellers in Asia could probably have enjoyed relatively peaceful and prosperous times under Domitian (1986 and 1990). A view similar to this has been accepted by Adela Yarbro Collins, who argues that there was no problem with Rome *per se*; instead, the problems facing the Christian communities of Asia were conflict with Jews, mutual antipathy towards neighbouring Gentiles and internal difficulties over wealth. Collins does, however, envisage the possibility of Roman magistrates being brought in to adjudicate disputes stimulated by such problems (Collins 1984: 84–110). Yet the more decisive evidence for the lack of oppression affecting the communities of Asia Minor is that there is simply no support for it in the letters to the seven churches. The letters are more helpful on this question than the visions in the latter part of the work because of their being written in discursive, not symbolical, language so that the difficulty of knowing whether a feature corresponds to some aspect of the actual experience of the author and his addressees or is part of the literary universe created in the work is far less severe. With respect to four of them, namely, Ephesus, Thyatira, Sardis and Laodicea, there is no reference whatever to any trouble being caused to those churches by Roman or civic authorities or by outsiders at all. Certainly, they have their problems. Thus, Ephesus is troubled by false apostles and by the

Nicolaitans (whose work John hates – 2.6) and they have lost their first love (2.4), but there is no reference to any present or impending crisis of external origin. Similarly, Thyatira is criticised for tolerating the works of the prophetess Jezebel, but she is plainly in or on the outskirts of the Christian community. As for Sardis and Laodicea, their problems are principally those of failing to keep the faith alive and they are not described as subject to any persecution.

In his letter to Pergamum, John does indeed note that the community in the city stayed firm when Antipas was martyred. But there is no reference to any anticipated persecution and it is unlikely that there was any general oppression in the past, since, if there had been, it would have been mentioned in the text rather than just the death of Antipas. The reference in the letter to 'the throne of Satan' (2.13) may be to the Roman imperial cult which was popular in the city, but there is no indication in the letter that it poses any present or future problems for the church there. In Philadelphia it would appear from the mention of the 'synagogue of Satan' that the local Jewish population was causing problems, although their nature is not specified. The only cloud on the horizon in this letter is not Roman persecution but the coming end of the world (3.11–12). Only with respect to Smyrna does John write of impending persecution, which will last for ten days, during the course of which some of the members of the community will be thrown into prison and, possibly, lose their lives. Once again, however, in this letter reference is made to the 'synagogue of Satan' and it may well be that he has in mind not persecution originating in Rome but a purely local event instigated by the Jewish community stirring up the civic authorities against the Christians, similar to incidents reported in Acts.

From this investigation we see that the issues which are most vexing the seer have little, if anything, to do with Rome. External pressure from the Jewish population appears to be present in Smyrna and Philadelphia, but what really seems to be agitating John are internal questions, disruption caused by false teaching, or false practice, or a general lukewarmness and falling away from the faith. Yet if Rome was not waging war on the saints, how are we able to account for the powerful anti-Roman mythopoesis created in the work? Adela Yarbro Collins is alive to this problem. She suggests that the cause underlying the composition of the work was the conflict between the Christian faith itself, as John understood it, and the social situation as he perceived it. She proposes that a new set of expectations had arisen out of faith in Jesus as the Messiah and from a belief that the Kingdom of God and Christ had been established. John was moved to write because of tension between his vision of the kingdom and his environment (1984: 106).

This is an attractive idea and certainly the prevalence of the imperial cult could well have been a matter of great concern to the author and his audience (Price 1984). David Aune has shown that in many respects the trappings of the heavenly court in the Apocalypse parallel but are superior to those of the emperor's court in Rome (1983). One consideration, however, leads me to hesitate in seeing Collins' type of explanation as persuasive, namely, the fact that in the letters the problem does not seem to be the environment so much as what was going on inside the congregations. On Collins' view there would be no real correspondence between what the text presents in the seven letters as the issues for the Christians of Asia Minor and the towering cycle of myth in which Rome is so thoroughly demonised in the second half of the work. What we need is an interpretation of the text which succeeds in explaining the connection between these two phenomena.

WITCHCRAFT AND SORCERY ACCUSATIONS: PERSPECTIVES FROM SOCIAL ANTHROPOLOGY

To assist in the exploration of this critical issue I propose to call in aid research conducted this century by social anthropologists into the phenomenon of witchcraft and sorcery accusations. To offer initial justification for what might seem at first a rather surprising step, it should be noted that at one point in the text Babylon, a form under which the beast parades from chapter 16 onwards, is directly accused of sorcery. This happens at 18.23 where it is said: 'all nations were deceived by your sorcery (*pharmakeia*)'. The same word or words cognate with it and having a similar meaning occur in three other places in Revelation (9.21, 21.8 and 22.15). There is only one other instance of *pharmakeia* or its cognates in the New Testament (Gal. 5.20). Given the lively discussion among anthropologists as to the meaning and function of witchcraft and sorcery and accusations of both among pre-literate peoples in our own time, the question arises as to whether the results of their investigations might shed some light on the attitude to Rome in the Apocalypse.

The natural starting point for the generation of a model of witchcraft and sorcery accusations is E.E. Evans-Pritchard's *Witchcraft, Oracles and Magic among the Azande* (1937 and 1976). Although the terms 'witchcraft' and 'sorcery' are roughly synonymous in ordinary English usage, among anthropologists they have acquired distinct meanings following Evans-Pritchard's discovery that the Azande distinguished between two different types of supernatural activities believed to occur in their midst. According to the Azande, a tribe from the southern Sudan, witchcraft consisted of a form of hereditary, psycho-physical power inherent in some persons. This power had the capacity to injure others without the aid of magical techniques and even though the witch was unaware of the harm he or she was causing. On the other hand, sorcerers did attain their ends by the use of magical techniques. As a general rule, sorcery was the use of magic for evil ends – typically to harm someone. But just as magic might be used as a sword, as it were, it could also be used defensively – as a shield against both sorcery and witchcraft.

Anthropologists have discovered that the distinction which Evans-Pritchard noticed the Azande drew between sorcery and witchcraft (with the witch causing harm without any of the paraphernalia of magic) is one found in many other pre-literate cultures, although it is by no means universal (Marwick 1986: 12–13). The phenomenon of the evil eye, which has existed in the Mediterranean area for millennia and was mentioned in Chapter 2, closely corresponds to the Azande notion of witchcraft (Douglas 1970: xxxvi; Murdock 1980: 58). G.P. Murdock has argued on the basis of a comprehensive ethnographic survey that the human societies which manifest a belief in witchcraft (and the evil eye) in this sense – at least to the extent that such beliefs are perceived to be a cause of illness – are concentrated in the circum-Mediterranean region, in certain adjacent areas of Africa and in parts of the Americas which have been influenced by the Spanish (1980: 57–8).

Magic among the Azande involves the use of objects and products obtained from trees and plants. Evans-Pritchard referred to these materials as 'medicines' (*ngua*). Among the Azande an important magical rite is normally accompanied by a spell (*sima*). The person performing the rite addresses the medicines and tells them what he or she wants them to do. There is no power in the words themselves; what is needed is that the medicines, which have a commission to carry out, know exactly what is required of them. Sometimes the Azande do not make a spell over the medicines, for example, when they are administering them as antidotes to persons believed to be victims of a sorcerer. The benign use of 'medicines' among the Azande covers a wide range of situations, including the treatment of illness, influencing rainfall, encouraging success in hunting or in love and ensuring safe journeys. The Azande do not distinguish strictly medicinal uses of 'medicines' from what we would regard as magical uses.

Evans-Pritchard found that witchcraft served three primary purposes among the Azande. First, it was seen as the cause of misfortune (especially sickness and accidents) which might befall someone. Secondly, witchcraft was thought to emanate from a witch who was motivated by hatred, envy, jealousy or greed toward the victim. Accordingly, an Azande in misfortune immediately began to give thought to the person most likely to hate him or her (1976: 45). Among the Azande, witches were believed only to injure people in the vicinity and the closer they were to their victims the more serious the attack. Evans-Pritchard considered that the reason for this belief was that people living at a distance from one another had insufficient social contacts to engender moral hatred. Thirdly, witchcraft comprised moral judgement. To say 'It is witchcraft' was virtually synonymous with saying 'It is bad.'

Among the Azande, Evans-Pritchard discovered, where many types of personal misfortune are attributed to witchcraft and sorcery, it is regarded as important to identify the witch responsible for causing a particular problem. Various methods are used for this purpose, the most highly regarded of which being the poison oracle. Under this technique, a person wishing to determine whether someone else is a witch names the suspect and then administers a particular form of poison to a hen. If the hen recovers, and the effect of the poison used is variable, the person is innocent. If the hen dies, the person named is the witch. Once the witch is identified, the victim sends an intermediary to him to convey the message that he has been identified by the oracle as the cause of the problem. This stage of the process constitutes the formal witchcraft accusation. The witch so accused almost invariably replies that he is not aware of harming anyone, but if he has, he is sorry and he beseeches the witchcraft in his stomach to become inactive. The entire affair is conducted with great courtesy – 'the whole point of the procedure is to put the witch in a good temper by being polite to him' (Evans-Pritchard 1976: 43). Although magic itself is often a private pursuit, accusations of sorcery or witchcraft are not; they are pre-eminently relational phenomena. As Max Marwick has noted, they involve the three separate roles of victim, accuser and accused (1986: 300–13). At times the victim and the accuser are one and the same person, although this not need be the case, as when the accuser is a friend or relative of the victim.

In his style of investigation Evans-Pritchard exhibited features of the functional analysis of his time, with its emphasis on understanding social systems in terms of homeostasis, or long-term equilibrium, and on examining the interdependence of institutions within a limited context of space and time, while largely ignoring the historical reasons which might have led to the emergence of those institutions. Thus he depicted witchcraft accusations as bringing grudges out into the open and defusing them, which served to maintain social stability. In the 1950s, however, some researchers began to focus on the manner in which the power of witchcraft accusations could be mobilised for the cyclical changes periodically undergone by the social system. This development paralleled a movement toward more conflict-oriented modes of analysis. In his study of the Cewa, Max Marwick showed that accusations of witchcraft and sorcery could actually be used as a 'social strain gauge', since they frequently occurred when a social group underwent fission, initially as rivals struggled for power within the group and later to confirm the split (Marwick 1965). From this perspective an accusation of witchcraft served not to cement social relationships but to fracture them (Douglas 1970: xxi).

The use of sorcery and witchcraft accusations in situations of conflict may be a substitute for physical forms of confrontation. Indeed, one possibility inherent in witchcraft accusations, to function as projected fantasy aggression, is delineated quite starkly among the Gusii, a Kenyan tribe. The Gusii, to a quite exceptional extent in the world at large, train their children not to engage in acts of aggression towards others. Such childhood training seems to have the effect that the Gusii resort to the use of private and verbal expressions of hostility rather than overt physical forms. The Gusii at times 'assault' their enemies by accusing them of hostile acts of witchcraft and sorcery for which they are simply retaliating in a verbal way. Thus, their early pattern of socialisation leads them to inhibit overt violence, but in substitution therefore to project their aggression onto others by indulging in fantasy aggression against them (LeVine 1963: 250–2).

One illuminating classification of witchcraft accusations devised by Mary Douglas (1970) focuses upon two questions: first, whether or not the accusation is made by an individual or is also taken up by the community and, secondly, whether the witch or sorcerer is perceived to be inside or outside the community. An accusation of witchcraft or sorcery made by a community will generally function to clarify and affirm social relations. The witch may be regarded as inside the community or outside it. Where a witch is perceived to be inside the community, he or she may be viewed as a member of a rival faction, in which case the accusation will serve to reinforce faction boundaries, or as a dangerous deviant, with the accusation functioning to control the deviant in the name of community values.

Examples of accusations of witchcraft made against outsiders have been found among the Navaho (Kluckhohn 1967), among the Lugbara in Africa (Middleton and Winter 1963) and in Oceania (Marwick 1986: 300–13). In this case the accusation serves to reaffirm the boundaries of the community *vis-à-vis* the outside world. Mary Douglas writes: 'The symbols of what we recognise across the globe as witchcraft all build on the theme of vulnerable internal goodness attacked by external power' (1970: xxvi). Or, as Middleton and Winter put it with reference to one tribe but having a wider application: 'The field of recognised obligations that compose the structure of the local community is defined in terms of the existence of sorcerers outside it and always threatening it, who deny the obligations of neighbourship' (1963: 273–4). Wherever strains within a community lead to outsiders being accused of witchcraft or sorcery it is clear that there is occurring a socially functional displacement of aggression from nearby persons to those outsiders. If the accusation were to be made against a member of one's own group, there is a danger that the resultant conflict might imperil the group's existence.

SORCERY ACCUSATIONS IN THE FIRST CENTURY

We find in Greek literature from Homer onwards a phenomenon similar to the medicines of the Azande, namely the use of *pharmaka* as a word to describe medicinal and magic drugs without discrimination. In the Circe incident in the Odyssey (10.213ff) the word *pharmakon* is used of the plant *moly* given to Odysseus by Hermes to counteract Circe's magic. The most potent wielder of *pharmaka* in the tradition was, of course, Medea (cf. Euripides' *Medea* 385). The Greek magical papyri are a rich source (Betz 1986). There is no doubt, although it is not possible to develop the argument here, that magic was prevalent in the first century. The various and proliferating corpora of curses (*defixiones*) and binding spells in Greek and Roman culture (see Faraone 1991: 3–32; Winkler 1991: 214–43) illustrate the frequency of magic aimed at harming or controlling others, in other words, of sorcery, of *pharmakeia*, a practice proscribed in Revelation at 9.21, 21.8 and 22.15 and in Gal. 5.20.

Although not so well explored, accusations of witchcraft and sorcery are also attested in the Graeco-Roman literature of this period. A good example occurs in Tacitus' *Annales* 2.69 where a senator was accused of having been responsible for the *defixiones* which allegedly killed Germanicus and was subsequently executed. At one point in Plutarch's *Moralia*, which is a good source for our purpose because of the stereotypical nature of the matters discussed, there appears the following account of an accusation of witchcraft made against the mistress of Philip of Macedon:

> King Philip was enamoured of a Thessalian woman who was accused of using magic charms upon him (*katapharmakeuein auton*). Olympias [Philip's wife] made haste to get the woman into her power. But when the latter had come into the queen's presence and was seen to be beautiful in appearance, and her conversation with the queen was not lacking in good-breeding or cleverness, Olympias exclaimed, 'Away with these slanders! You have magic charms (*pharmaka*) in yourself.
>
> (*Moralia* 141B; Babbitt 1962: 315)

A more malign incident is recorded with respect to the tyrant Dionysius the Elder. Finding that Aristomache, one of his two wives, was barren, Dionysius accused the mother of his other wife of practising sorcery against her (*katapharmakeuein*) and put her to death (Plutarch, *Dion* III.3).

There is even explicit ancient testimony to the effect that it is better to express one's aggression against outsiders than against insiders. At one point in his *Moralia* Plutarch says:

> Since all human nature bears its crop of contention, jealousy, envy, 'boon-comrade of rattle-brained men', as Pindar says, a man would profit in no moderate degree by venting those emotions on his enemies and turning the course of such discharges, so to speak, as far away as possible from his associates and relatives.
>
> (*Moralia* 89F; Babbitt 1962: 35)

He then proceeds to cite the example of a statesman from the island of Chios named Demus who, when he found himself on the winning side of some civil strife there, put this principle into effect by advising his party associates not to banish all their opponents but to leave some of them behind as useful targets for negative emotions. This data reveals that in the first century Greco-Roman world there existed attitudes and practices with respect to sorcery and accusations of sorcery analogous to the phenomena examined by anthropologists in contemporary pre-industrial settings. There is, accordingly, a demonstrable ancient context, at least in general terms, for what we find in Revelation 18.23.

SORCERY ACCUSATIONS IN THE APOCALYPSE

Sorcery accusation actually figures much earlier in the work, however. In the letter to Thyatira it is said: 'But I have this against you, that you tolerate the woman Jezebel, who calls herself a prophetess and teaches and misleads my servants to practise incest (*porneusai*) and to eat meat sacrificed to idols' (2.20; my translation). This statement constitutes an implied accusation that the woman has engaged in sorcery, at least at a metaphorical level. The basis for this view is that in the Old Testament Jezebel, Ahab's wife, is unequivocally accused of both *pharmakeia* and *porneia* at 2 Kings 9.22. In the terms of Mary Douglas' classification discussed above, this statement constitutes a sorcery accusation made against an insider to label and condemn her as a deviant in the name of certain community values, namely, those concerned with the degrees of intermarriage permitted among relatives and the question of whether one could eat meat originating in pagan sacrifices. In this instance the accusation can be interpreted using conflict analysis as a 'social strain gauge'.

The most explicit material in the text to which *pharmakeia* at 18.23 refers is found in the description of the various devices, plainly magical or pseudo-magical in nature, which the beast from the earth employs to induce the inhabitants of the earth to worship its master:

> It worked great miracles, even making fire come down from heaven to earth where people could see it. By the miracles it was allowed to perform in the presence of the beast it deluded the inhabitants of the earth, and persuaded them to erect an image in honour of the beast which had been wounded by the sword and yet lived. It was allowed to give breath to the image of the beast so that it could even speak . . . (13.14–15a; *NEB*)

Underlying this description appear to be magical, or rather pseudo-magical, practices employed in connection with the imperial cult, as described in a recent article by Steven J. Scherrer (1984). Sorcery practised in the imperial cult provides the ultimate foundation for the accusation of Babylon's *pharmakeia* deceiving the nations of the earth at 18.23. Yet it is in the presentation of Babylon as harlot , as *porne*, in chapters 17 and 18 that the importance of sorcery accusations to the author becomes most apparent. For the Old Testament at times links *porneia*, which is a significant attribute of Babylon in the Apocalypse, with sorcery when it is ascribed to a non-Israelite person or city. Such is the case with Nineveh in Nahum 3.4 and, more importantly, Babylon in Isaiah 47.

We may now seek to explain the function of the anti-Roman mythopoesis in the work using the witchcraft accusation perspectives developed above. Our explanation will address the necessity of explaining why Rome, when it is not actually a threat to the communities, should be so totally demonised. The author perceives the communities to whom he writes as being subjected to various forms of strain. Thus the Nicolaitans are engaging in some unspecified form of malpractice in Ephesus (2.7) and erroneous teaching in Pergamum (2.15). Jezebel is a problem in Thyatira. False apostles have been causing difficulties in Ephesus (2.2). Enthusiasm for the faith is dying in Sardis (3.1–3), while in Laodicea, excessive prosperity has led to the Christians there becoming lukewarm (3.15). Even what appears to be external opposition from the Jews in Philadelphia (3.9) and Smyrna (2.9) may have an internal cause, namely, hostility aroused by the Christian practice of eating profane food in consequence of the teaching of people such as Jezebel. In a number of churches, therefore, there have been tensions and ambiguities in relation-ships. Some of these tensions have been generated by a debate over authority. This is the case with Jezebel's claim, plainly dis-puted by John, to be a prophetess and of the very similar expression used of the false apostles (2.2). Accordingly, the author is writing in a situation of strain in the social structure of some of the churches of Asia and a general diminution of faith in others. He must frame a reply to this malaise and at the same time legitimate, that is, explain and justify, his vision of the faith and its future.

A significant part of the author's response to this situation is to project before the readers of the text a powerful cycle of myth in which Rome features as a beast in league with Satan, having a murderous enmity towards Christians and constituting a princi-pal cause of their woes. But Rome is not, in fact, a source of any great difficulty for the Christian communities of Asia at this time. Rather it functions in the cycle of myth created in the work as a scapegoat for problems which are largely internal to the seven congregations. That Rome is depicted in this way in the Apoc-alypse permits us to draw comparisons with groups such as the Navaho and the Lugbara which lay the blame for internal misfor-tune upon witches or sorcerers outside their boundaries. To say this is not to deny that there were aspects to the recollection or experience of the Christians of Asia which went some way towards making antipathy to Rome credible: both the Neronian persecu-tion and the prevalence of the imperial cult in Asia Minor provided justification for a negative image of Rome. The latter factor, in particular, provided a strong theological reason. The point remains, however, that there is a noticeable lack of propor-tion between the actual impact such factors were having on the communities of Asia and the extent to which Rome is portrayed in the work as the epitome of evil. These factors should be seen, therefore, as spurs to the author's prophetic imagination whereas the actual reason for such a presentation of Rome lies elsewhere – within the communities to which the work was directed and with respect to whose difficulties a sorcery accusation of this type might fulfil a valuable social function.

To refer to Mary Douglas' classification, what we witness here is the phenomenon of a witchcraft accusation being launched against an entity outside the community. Such an accusation serves to reaffirm the identity of the community on whose behalf the accusation is made in relation to the outside world. As noted above, the Gusii of Kenya, who encourage severe inhibition of physical violence, engage in witchcraft accusations as a form of fantasy aggression. This practice provides a useful analogy to the treatment of Rome in the Apocalypse. The hostility which might otherwise be vented upon all members of the local communities who are causing difficulties is redirected in the form of an elaborate aggressive fantasy onto Rome as, in part, sorcerer. One result of this approach is to avoid the possibility of the communities fracturing if too many members were so accused. That there are limits to how far the text will go in denouncing insiders emerges in the case of Jezebel, the one person who is charged (albeit by implication) with sorcery, since there is no suggestion that she should be expelled from the congregation. Although the ambit and emphasis of the sorcery accusation go far beyond the facts of Rome's impact on the Christians of the seven cities, the capacity of the author to exaggerate the forces of evil arrayed against them is evident, as already noted, from the way he presents their involvement in the fall of Satan in 12.10–11.

The primary function of portraying Rome as a sorcerer is to clarify and reaffirm the identity of the communities both in relation to the outside world and in response to internal tendencies toward disintegration and ennui. By directing an accusation of sorcery at an entity presented (however unjustifiably) as a common threat and as an actor in a vast, cosmological drama the author adopts a strategy which emphasises the shared experience and the shared destiny of the churches of Asia and thereby counteracts tendencies towards error or lassitude among them. What we find in Revelation, therefore, is not the 'product of a perfervid and psychotic imagination' but rather a socially functional displacement of aggression from troublesome insiders to an outside sorcery figure – Rome.

References

Abelson, R.P. *et al.* (eds) (1968) *Theories of Cognitive Dissonance: A Sourcebook*. Chicago: Rand McNally.

Aberle, David F. (1970) 'A Note on Relative Deprivation Theory as Applied to Millenarian and Other Cult Movements', in Thrupp 1970: 209–14.

Ashton, John (ed.) (1986) *The Interpretation of John*. Philadelphia and London: Fortress Press and SPCK.

—— (1991) *Understanding the Fourth Gospel*. Oxford: Clarendon Press.

Aune, David E. (1983) 'The Influence of Roman Imperial Court Ceremonial on the Apocalypse of John', *Biblical Research* 28: 5–26.

Babbitt, Frank Cole (1962) *Plutarch's Moralia*. Volume II (88B–171F). Loeb edition. London and Cambridge, Mass.: William Heinemann.

Bahat, D. (1970) *Jerusalem – Its Epochs*. Jerusalem.

Barrett, C.K. (1959) 'The Background of Mark 10:45', in A.J.B. Higgins ed., *New Testament Essays: Studies in Memory of Thomas Walter Manson 1893–1958*. Manchester: Manchester University Press, 1–18.

—— (1978) *The Gospel According to St John: An Introduction with Commentary and Notes on the Greek Text*. Second edition. London: SPCK.

Barrett, David (1968) *Schism and Renewal in Africa: An Analysis of Six Thousand Contemporary Religious Movements*. Nairobi: Oxford University Press.

Barton, Stephen (1992) 'The Communal Dimension of Earliest Christianity: A Critical Survey of the Field', *Journal of Theological Studies* 43: 399–427.

Bartsch, Hans Werner (ed.) (1964) *Kerygma and Myth: A Theological Debate*, Eng. trans. by R.H. Fuller. Volume I. London: SPK.

Berger, Peter L. (1969 [1967]) *The Sacred Canopy: Elements of a Sociological Theory of Religion*. New York: Anchor.

Berger, Peter L. and Luckmann, Thomas (1984 [1966]) *The Social Construction of Reality: A Treatise in the Sociology of Knowledge*. London: Pelican.

Betz, Hans Dieter (1975) 'The Literary Composition and Function of Paul's Letter to the Galatians', *New Testament Studies* 21: 353–79.

—— (1979) *Galatians: A Commentary on Paul's Letter to the Churches in Galatia*. Philadelphia: Fortress Press.

—— (ed.) (1986) *The Greek Magical Papyri in Translation, Including the Demotic Spells*. Volume One: Texts. Chicago and London: University of Chicago Press.

Black, Max (1962) *Models and Metaphors*. Ithaca, NY: Cornell University Press.

—— (1979) 'More about Metaphor', in Anthony Ortony (ed.), *Metaphor and Thought*. Cambridge: Cambridge University Press, 19–43.

Bourdieu, Pierre (1965) 'The Sentiment of Honour in Kabyle Society', in Peristiany 1965: 191–241.

Breech, E. (1973) 'These Fragments I Have Shored against My Ruins: The Form and Function of 4 Ezra', *Journal of Biblical Literature* 92: 267–74.

Brown, Peter (1972) *Religion and Society in the Age of Saint Augustine*. London: Faber & Faber.

Bultmann, Rudolf (1964) 'New Testament and Mythology', in Bartsch 1964: 1–16.

Burridge, Kenelm (1969) *New Heaven, New Earth: A Study of Millenarian Activities*. Oxford: Basil Blackwell.

Burton, Sir Richard F. (1964) *Personal Narrative of a Pilgrimage to Al–Madinah & Meccah*. Two volumes. New York: Dover Publications.

Campbell, J.K. (1964) *Honour, Family and Patronage: A Study of Institutions and Moral Values in a Greek Mountain Community*. New York and Oxford: Oxford University Press.

Capper, Brian (1983) 'The Interpretation of Acts 5.4', *Journal for the Study of the New Testament* 19: 117–31.

Carney, Thomas F. (1975) *The Shape of the Past: Models and Antiquity*. Lawrence, Kans.: Coronado Press.

Carroll, Robert P. (1979) *When Prophecy Fails: Reactions and Responses to Failure in the Old Testament Prophetic Traditions*. London: SCM Press.

—— (1989) 'Prophecy and Society', in Clements 1989: 203–25.

Casey, M. (1986) Review of John J. Collins, *Daniel, with an Introduction to Apocalyptic Literature*, in *Journal of Theological Studies* 37: 478–84.

Charlesworth, James H. (ed.) (1990) *John and the Dead Sea Scrolls*. New York: Crossroad.

Clements, R.E. (ed.) (1989) *The World of Ancient Israel: Sociological, Anthropological and Political Perspectives: Essays by Members of the Society for Old Testament Study*. Cambridge: Cambridge University Press.

Cohn, Norman (1970) *The Pursuit of the Millennium: Revolutionary Millenarians and Mystical Anarchists in the Middle Ages*. London: Temple Smith.

Collins, Adela Yarbro (1976) *The Combat Myth in the Book of Revelation*. Missoula, Mont.: Scholars Press.

—— (1984) *Crisis & Catharsis: The Power of the Apocalypse*. Philadelphia: Westminster Press.

Collins, John J. (1977) *The Apocalyptic Vision of the Book of Daniel*. Chico, Calif.: Scholars Press.

—— (1978) 'Introduction: Towards the Morphology of a Genre', *Semeia* 14: 1–20.

—— (1987) *The Apocalyptic Imagination: An Introduction to the Jewish Matrix of Christianity*. New York: Crossroad.

Conzelmann, Hans (1975) *1 Corinthians: A Commentary on the First Epistle to the Corinthians*. Philadelphia: Fortress Press.

Cross, F.M., Lemke, W.E. and Miller, P.D. Jnr (eds.) (1976) *Magnalia Dei: Essays on the Bible and Archaeology in Memory of G. Ernest Wright*. Garden City, NY: Doubleday.

Currie, Stuart D. (1986) 'Speaking in Tongues: Early Evidence Outside the New Testament Bearing on *Glōssais Lalein*', in Mills 1986: 83–106.

Darr, John (1992) *On Character Building: The Reader and the Rhetoric of Characterization in Luke-Acts*. Louisville, Ky.: Westminster Press/John Knox.

Davies, J.D. (1952) 'Pentecost and Glossolalia', *Journal of Theological Studies* n.s. 3: 228–31.

Davies, Philip R. (1982) *The Damascus Covenant: An Interpretation of the 'Damascus Document'*. Sheffield: JSOT Press.

—— (1989) 'The Social World of the Apocalyptic Writings', in Clements 1989: 251–71.

Defoe, Daniel (1987 [1719]) *Robinson Crusoe*. Oxford and New York: Oxford University Press.

Di Lella, Alexander A. (1977) 'The One in Human Likeness and the Holy Ones of the Most High in Daniel 7', *Catholic Biblical Quarterly* 39: 1–19.

Donceel-Voûte, Pauline (1992) 'The Archaeology of Khirbet Qumran', paper given in New York at the New York Academy of Sciences on 14 December.

Douglas, Mary (1966) *Purity and Danger: An Analysis of Concepts of Pollution and Taboo*. London: Routledge & Kegan Paul.

—— (1970) *Witchcraft Confessions and Accusations*. London: Tavistock Publications.

Dunn, J.D.G. (1983) 'The Incident at Antioch (Gal. 2:11–18)'. *Journal for the Study of the New Testament* 18: 3–57, reprinted in Dunn 1990: 129–81, together with responses to reactions thereon.

—— (1990) *Jesus, Paul and the Law*. London: SPCK.

—— (1991) *The Partings of the Ways between Christianity and Judaism and their Significance for the Character of Christianity*. London and Philadelphia: SCM Press and Trinity Press International.

Durkheim, Emile (1976 [1912]) *The Elementary Forms of the Religious Life*. Eng. trans. by J.W. Swain. Second edition. London: George Allen & Unwin.

Eliade, Mircea (1989 [1954]) *The Myth of the Eternal Return*. Eng. trans. by W.R. Trask. London: Penguin.

Elliott, John H. (1988) 'The Fear of the Leer: The Evil Eye from the Bible to Li'l Abner', *Forum* 4: 42–71.

—— (1990) 'Paul, Galatians, and the Evil Eye', *Currents in Theology and Mission* 17: 262–73.

Esler, Philip F. (1987) *Community and Gospel in Luke-Acts: The Social and Political Motivations of Lucan Theology*. Cambridge: Cambridge University Press.

—— (1992) 'Glossolalia and the Admission of Gentiles into the Early Christian Community', *Biblical Theology Bulletin* 22: 136–42.

—— (1993a) Review of Overman 1990, in *Biblical Interpretation* 1: 255–8.

—— (1993b) Review of Neyrey 1991, in *Biblical Interpretation* 1: 250–5.

—— (1994a) 'The Social Function of 4 Ezra', *Journal for the Study of the New Testament* 53: 99–123.

—— (1994b) Review of Darr 1992, in *Biblical Interpretation* 2: forthcoming.

—— (1994c) Review of Hill 1992, in *Biblical Interpretation* 2: forthcoming.

Evans-Pritchard, E.E. (1937) *Witchcraft, Oracles and Magic among the Azande*. Oxford: Clarendon Press.

—— (1976) *Witchcraft, Oracles and Magic among the Azande*. A version of Evans-Pritchard 1937 abridged and introduced by E. Gillies. Oxford: Clarendon Press.

Faraone, Christopher A. (1991) 'The Agonistic Context of Early Greek Binding Spells', in Faraone and Obbink 1991: 3–32.

Faraone, Christopher A. and Obbink, Dirk (eds.) (1991) *Magika Hiera: Ancient Greek Magic & Religion*. New York and Oxford: Oxford University Press.

Fenton, William N. (1968) *Parker on the Iroquois*. Syracuse, NY: Syracuse University Press.

Festinger, Leon (1957) *A Theory of Cognitive Dissonance*. Evanston, Ill., and White Plains, NY: Peterson & Co.

Fiorenza, Elizabeth Schüssler (1985) *The Book of Revelation: Justice and Judgment*. Philadelphia: Fortress Press.

Forbes, Christopher (1987) 'Prophecy and Inspired Speech in Early Christianity and its Hellenistic Environment', Macquarie University PhD thesis being prepared for publication in the Wissenschaftliche Untersuchungen zum Neuen Testament series. Tübingen: J.C.B. Mohr (Paul Siebeck).

Forsyth, Neil (1987) *The Old Enemy: Satan and the Combat Myth*. Princeton, NJ: Princeton University Press.

Fortna, Robert T. and Gaventa, Beverly R. (eds.) (1990) *The Conversation Continues: Studies in Paul & John in Honor of J. Louis Martyn*. Nashville: Abingdon.

Fustel de Coulanges, Numa Denis (undated [1864]) *The Ancient City: A Study on the Religion, Laws, and Institutions of Greece and Rome*. Garden City, NY: Doubleday Anchor.

Gadamer, Hans-Georg (1979) *Truth and Method*. London: Sheed & Ward. Second edition. Eng. trans. by William Glen-Doepel of the second (1965) German edition.

Gager, John (1975) *Kingdom and Community: The Social World of Early Christianity*. Englewood Cliffs, NJ: Prentice-Hall.

Gasque, Ward W. (1975) *A History of the Criticism of the Acts of the Apostles*. Grand Rapids, Mich.: W.B. Eerdmans Publishing Co.

Gerth, H.H. and Mills, C. Wright (1970) *From Max Weber: Essays in Sociology*. London: Routledge & Kegan Paul.

Golb, N. (1980) 'The Problem of Origin and Identification of the Dead Sea Scrolls', *Proceedings of the American Philosophical Society* 124: 1–24.

—— (1985) 'Who Hid the Dead Sea Scrolls?', *Biblical Archaeology* 48: 68–82.

Goodman, Felicitas D. (1972) *Speaking in Tongues: A Cross-Cultural Study of Glossolalia*. Chicago: University of Chicago Press.

Grabbe, Lester (1989) 'The Social Setting of Early Jewish Apocalypticism', *Journal for the Study of Pseudepigrapha* 4: 24–47.

Haenchen, E. (1971) *The Acts of the Apostles*. Oxford: Basil Blackwell.

Harrington, Daniel J. (1988) *The Maccabean Revolt: Anatomy of a Biblical Revolution*. Wilmington, Del.: Michael Glazier.

Hellholm, David (ed.) (1989) *Apocalypticism in the Mediterranean World and the Near East*. Second edition. Tübingen: J.C.B. Mohr (Paul Siebeck).

Hengel, Martin, in collaboration with Roland Deines (1991) *The Pre-Christian Paul*. London and Philadelphia: SCM Press and Trinity Press International.

Hester, James D. (1984) 'The Rhetorical Structure of Galatians 1:11–2:14', *Journal of Biblical Literature* 103: 223–33.

Hill, Christopher (1985) *The World Turned Upside Down: Radical Ideas during the English Revolution*. London: Penguin.

Hill, Craig C. (1992) *Hebrews and Hellenists: Reappraising Division within the Earliest Church*. Minneapolis: Fortress Press.

Holmberg, Bengt (1978) *Paul and Power: The Structure of Authority in the Primitive Church as Reflected in the Pauline Epistles*. Lund: Studentlitteratur.

—— (1990) *Sociology and the New Testament: An Appraisal*. Minneapolis: Fortress Press.

Howard, George (1979) *Paul: Crisis in Galatia: A Study in Early Christian Theology*. Cambridge: Cambridge University Press.

Isenberg, Sheldon R. (1974) 'Millenarism in Greco-Roman Palestine', *Religion* 4: 26–46.

Kennedy, George A. (1984) *New Testament Interpretation through Rhetorical Criticism*. Chapel Hill, NC, and London: University of North Carolina Press.

Kildahl, J.P. (1972) *The Psychology of Speaking in Tongues*. New York: Harper & Row.

Kluckhohn, Clyde (1967) *Navaho Witchcraft*. Boston: Beacon Press.

Knibb, Michael A. (1983) 'Apocalyptic and Wisdom in 4 Ezra', *Journal for the Study of Judaism* 13: 56–72.

—— (1987) *The Qumran Community*. Cambridge: Cambridge University Press.

Koch, K. (1972) *The Rediscovery of Apocalyptic*. Eng. trans. by M. Kohl of 1970 German original. London: SCM Press.

Kümmel, Werner Georg (1978) *The New Testament: The History of the Investigation of its Problems*. Eng. trans. by S. McLean Gilmour and Howard C. Kee of 1970 German original. London: SCM Press.

La Barre, Weston (1978) *The Ghost Dance: The Origins of Religion*. New York: Del Publishing Co.

Le Vine, Robert A. (1963) 'Witchcraft and Sorcery in a Gusii Community', in Middleton 1963: 221–55.

Lindars, Barnabas (1991) *The Theology of the Letter to the Hebrews*. Cambridge: Cambridge University Press.

MacDonald, William G. (1986) 'Glossolalia in the New Testament', in Mills 1986: 127–40.

MacIntyre, Alasdair (1981) *After Virtue: A Study in Moral Theory*. London: Duckworth.

Malherbe, Abraham J. (1986) *Moral Exhortation: A Greco-Roman Sourcebook*. Philadelphia: Fortress Press.
—— (1987) *Paul and the Thessalonians: The Philosophic Tradition of Pastoral Care*. Philadelphia: Fortress Press.
Malina, Bruce J. (1981) *The New Testament World: Insights from Cultural Anthropology*. London: SCM Press.
—— (1986) 'Normative Dissonance and Christian Origins', *Semeia* 35: 35–59.
—— (1989) 'Christ and Time: Swiss or Mediterranean?', *Catholic Biblical Quarterly* 51: 1–31.
Malina, Bruce J. and Neyrey, Jerome H. (1988) *Calling Jesus Names: The Social Value of Labels in Matthew*. Sonoma, Calif.: Polebridge.
—— (1991) 'Conflict in Luke–Acts: Labelling and Deviance Theory', in Neyrey 1991: 97–122.
Malinowski, Bruno (1948) 'Myth in Primitive Psychology', in his *Magic, Science and Religion and Other Essays*. Garden City, NY: Anchor, 93–148.
Malouf, David (1980) *An Imaginary Life*. London: Picador.
Martyn, J. Louis (1979 [1968]) *History and Theology in the Fourth Gospel*. Second edition. Nashville: Abingdon.
Marwick, Max (1965) *Sorcery in its Social Setting*. Manchester: Manchester University Press.
—— (ed.) (1986) *Witchcraft and Sorcery*. Second edition. London: Penguin.
Marx, Karl and Engels, Friedrich (1963) *The German Ideology*. New York: International Publishers Co.
May, L. Carlyle (1956) 'A Survey of Glossolalia and Related Phenomena in Non–Christian Religions', *American Anthropologist* 58: 75–86; reprinted in Mills 1986: 53–82.
Meeks, Wayne A. (1972) 'The Man from Heaven in Johannine Sectarianism', *Journal of Biblical Literature* 91: 44–72, reprinted in Ashton 1986: 141–73.
—— (1983) *The First Urban Christians: The Social World of the Apostle Paul*. New Haven and London: Yale University Press.
Middleton, John and Winter, E.H. (eds.) (1963) *Witchcraft and Sorcery in East Africa*. London: Routledge & Kegan Paul.
Mills, Watson E. (ed.) (1986) *Speaking in Tongues: A Guide to Research on Glossolalia*. Grand Rapids, Mich.: W.B. Eerdmans Publishing Co.
Moule, C.D.F. (1982) 'Neglected Features in the Problem of the Son of Man', in his *Essays in New Testament Interpretation*. Cambridge: Cambridge University Press, 75–90.
Moxnes, Halvor (1988) *The Economy of the Kingdom: Social Conflict and Economic Relations in Luke's Gospel*. Philadelphia: Fortress Press.
—— (1991) 'Patron–Client Relations and the New Community in Luke–Acts', in Neyrey 1991: 241–68.
Munn, Nancy D. (1992) 'The Cultural Anthropology of Time: A Critical Essay', *Annual Review of Anthropology* 21: 93–123.
Murdock, George P. (1980) *Theories of Illness: A World Survey*. Pittsburgh: Pittsburgh University Press.

Neusner, J., Green, W.S. and Frerichs, E.S. (eds.) (1987) *Judaisms and Their Messiahs at the Turn of the Christian Era*. Cambridge: Cambridge University Press.

Neyrey, Jerome H. (1988) 'Bewitched in Galatia: Paul and Cultural Anthropology', *Catholic Biblical Quarterly* 50: 72–100.

—— (1990) 'Honor and Shame: Pivotal Values in 1 Corinthians', paper given at a meeting of the Context Group in Portland, Oregon.

—— (ed.) (1991) *The Social World of Luke–Acts: Models for Interpretation*. Peabody, Mass.: Hendrickson.

Nineham, Dennis (1978) *The Use and Abuse of the Bible: A Study of the Bible in an Age of Rapid Cultural Change*. London: SPCK.

Noth, Martin (1966) 'The Holy Ones of the Most High', in his *The Laws in the Pentateuch and Other Studies*. Edinburgh and London: Oliver & Boyd, 215–28.

Oakman, Douglas E. (1991) 'The Countryside in Luke–Acts', in Neyrey 1991: 151–79.

Overholt, Thomas W. (1986) *Prophecy in Cross-Cultural Perspective: A Sourcebook for Biblical Researchers*. Atlanta, Ga.: Scholars Press.

Overman, J. Andrew (1990) *Matthew's Gospel and Formative Judaism: The Social World of the Matthean Community*. Minneapolis: Fortress Press.

Parker, Arthur C. (1913) *The Code of Handsome Lake*. Albany, NY: State Museum.

Peristiany, J.G. (ed.) (1965) *Honour and Shame: The Values of Mediterranean Society*. London: Weidenfeld & Nicolson.

Peristiany, J.G. and Pitt-Rivers, Julian, eds. (1992) *Honor and Grace in Anthropology*. Cambridge: Cambridge University Press.

Pitt-Rivers, Julian (1961) *The People of the Sierra*. Chicago: University of Chicago Press.

—— (ed.) (1963) *Mediterranean Countrymen: Essays in the Social Anthropology of the Mediterranean*. Paris and La Haye: Mouton & Co.

—— (1965) 'Honour and Social Status', in Peristiany 1965: 19–77.

—— (1977) *The Fate of Shechem or the Politics of Sex: Essays in the Anthropology of the Mediterranean*. Cambridge: Cambridge University Press.

Pixner, Bargil (1983) 'Unravelling the Copper Scroll: A Study on the Topography of 3Q15', *Revue de Qumran* 11: 323–65, at 342–47 and 363.

Porter, P. A. (1983) *Metaphors and Monsters: A Literary–Critical Study of Daniel 7 and 8*. Lund: CWK Gleerup.

Porton, Gary G. (1988) *Goyim: Gentiles and Israelites in Mishnah-Tosefta*. Atlanta, Ga: Scholars Press.

Price, Simon R.F. (1984) *Rituals and Power: The Roman Imperial Cult in Asia Minor*. Cambridge: Cambridge University Press.

Rabin, Chaim (1954) *The Zadokite Documents: I The Admonitions. II The Laws*. Oxford: Clarendon Press.

Räisänen, Heikki (1990) *Beyond New Testament Theology: A Story and a Programme*. London and Philadelphia: SCM Press and Trinity Press International.

Reid, Stephen Breck (1989) *Enoch and Daniel: A Form Critical and Sociological Study of Historical Apocalypses*. Berkeley, Calif.: Bibal Press.

Rensberger, David (1989) *Overcoming the World: Politics and Community in the Gospel of John*. London: SPCK.

Ribeiro, Rene (1970) 'Brazilian Messianic Movements', in Thrupp 1970: 55–69.

Rice, P. and Waugh, P. (1990) *Modern Literary Theory: A Reader*. London: Edward Arnold.

Robinson, J.A.T. (1976) *Redating the New Testament*. Philadelphia: Westminster Press.

Rohrbaugh, Richard L. (1991) 'The Pre-Industrial City in Luke-Acts: Urban Social Relations', in Neyrey 1991: 125–49.

Roll, Eric (1973) *A History of Economic Thought*. Fourth edition. London: Faber & Faber.

Rowland, Christopher (1985) *The Open Heaven: A Study of Apocalyptic in Judaism and Early Christianity*. London: SPCK.

—— (1988) *Radical Christianity: A Reading of Recovery*. Cambridge: Polity Press.

Salo, Kalervo (1991) *Luke's Treatment of the Law: A Redaction-Critical Investigation*. Helsinki: Suomalainen Tiedeakatemia.

Samarin, W.J. (1972) *Tongues of Men and Angels: The Religious Language of Pentecostalism*. New York: Macmillan Co.

Sanders, E.P. (1977) *Paul and Palestinian Judaism: A Comparison of Patterns of Religion*. Philadelphia: Fortress Press.

—— (1989) 'The Genre of Palestinian Jewish Apocalypses', in Hellholm 1989: 447–59.

—— (1990) 'Jewish Association with Gentiles and Galatians 2.1–14', in Fortna and Gaventa 1990: 170–88.

Schechter, S. (1910) *Documents of Jewish Sectaries. Vol. I: Fragments of a Zadokite Work*. Cambridge: Cambridge University Press.

Scheler, Max (ed.) (1924) *Versuche zu einer Soziologie des Wissens*. Munich: Duncker & Humblot.

Scherrer, Steven J. (1984) 'Signs and Wonders in the Imperial Cult: A New Look at a Roman Religious Institution in the Light of Rev. 13: 13–15', *Journal of Biblical Literature* 104: 599–610.

Schiffman, Lawrence H. (1989) *The Eschatological Community of the Dead Sea Scrolls: A Study of the Rule of the Congregation*. Atlanta, Ga: Scholars Press.

Schwimmer, Erik (ed.) (1976) *Francis Edgar Williams. 'The Vailala Madness' and Other Essays*. St Lucia, Queensland: University of Queensland Press.

Segal, Alan F. (1990) *Paul the Convert: The Apostolate and Apostasy of Saul the Pharisee*. New Haven and London: Yale University Press.

Sharpe, Eric (1975) *Comparative Religion: A History*. London: Duckworth.

Smith, Robertson W. (1956 [1889]) *The Religion of the Semites: The Fundamental Institutions*. New York: Meridian.

Squires, John T. (1993) *The Plan of God in Luke-Acts*. Society for New Testament Studies Monograph Series No. 76. Cambridge: Cambridge University Press.

Stanton, Graham (1992) *A Gospel for a New People: Studies in Matthew*. Edinburgh: T. & T. Clark.

Steinbeck, John (1975 [1939]) *The Grapes of Wrath*. London: Pan Books.

Stendahl, Krister (1963) 'The Apostle Paul and the Introspective Conscience of the West', *Harvard Theological Review* 56: 199–215, reprinted
in his *Paul among Jews and Gentiles and Other Essays*. London: SCM Press,
1977, 78–96.
Stone, Michael Edward (1976) 'Lists of Revealed Things in the Apocalyptic Literature', in Cross *et al.* 1976: 414–52.
—— (1987) 'The Question of the Messiah in 4 Ezra', in Neusner *et al.*
1987: 209–224.
—— (1990) *Fourth Ezra: A Commentary on the Book of Fourth Ezra*. Minneapolis: Fortress Press.
Theissen, Gerd (1987) *Psychological Aspects of Pauline Theology*. Edinburgh: T. & T. Clark.
Thompson, A.L. (1977) *Responsibility for Evil in the Theodicy of 4 Ezra*.
Society of Biblical Literature Dissertation Series No. 29. Missoula,
Mont.: Scholars Press.
Thompson, Leonard L. (1986) 'A Sociological Analysis of Tribulation in
the Apocalypse of John', *Semeia* 36: 147–74.
—— (1990) *The Book of Revelation: Apocalypse and Empire*. New York and
Oxford: Oxford University Press.
Thrupp, Sylvia L. (ed.) (1970) *Millennial Dreams in Action: Studies in
Revolutionary Religious Movements*. New York: Schocken Books.
Tolbert, Mary Ann (1989) *Sowing the Gospel: Mark's World in
Literary-Historical Perspective*. Minneapolis: Fortress Press.
Van Gennep, Arnold (1960) *The Rites of Passage*. Eng. trans. by Monika B.
Vizedom and Gabrielle L. Caffee. Chicago: University of Chicago
Press.
Vaux, Roland de (1973) *Archaeology and the Dead Sea Scrolls*. London:
Oxford University Press.
Vermes, Geza (1975) *The Dead Sea Scrolls in English*. Second edition.
London: Penguin.
Vermes, Geza and Goodman, Martin D. (1989) *The Essenes According to the
Classical Sources*. Sheffield: JSOT Press.
Verseput, D.J. (1993) 'Paul's Gentile Mission and the Jewish Christian
Community: A Study of the Narrative in Galatians 2 and 3', *New
Testament Studies* 39: 36–58.
Wallace, Anthony F.C. (1970) *The Death and Rebirth of the Seneca*. New
York: Alfred A. Knopf.
Watson, Francis (1986) *Paul, Judaism and the Gentiles: A Sociological
Approach*. Cambridge: Cambridge University Press.
Williams, C.G. (1981) *Tongues of the Spirit: A Study of Pentecostal Glossolalia
and Related Phenomena*. Cardiff: University of Wales Press.
Williams, Francis Edgar (1976) 'The Vailala Madness' and 'The Vailala
Madness in Retrospect', in Schwimmer 1976: 331–84 and 385–95.
Wilson, Bryan R. (1975) *Magic and the Millennium*. London: Paladin.
Wilson, Robert R. (1980) *Prophecy and Society in Ancient Israel*. Phila-
delphia: Fortress Press.
Winkler, John J. (1991) 'The Constraints of Eros', in Faraone and Obbink
1991: 214–43.
Worsley, Peter (1970) *The Trumpet Shall Sound: A Study of 'Cargo' Cults in
Melanesia*. London: Paladin.

Wuthnow, Robert, Hunter, James D., Bergesen, Albert and Kurzweil, Edith (1987) *Cultural Analysis: The Work of Peter L. Berger, Mary Douglas, Michel Foucault and Juergen Habermas.* London and New York: Routledge & Kegan Paul.

Index of ancient sources

Index of modern authors